Cabin Crew
Interview
Made Easy

This page has been intentionally left blank

TOP SECRETS
Revealed

The
Cabin Crew
Interview
Made Easy

The Ultimate Edition by
Caitlyn Rogers

Published by
Aspire Publishing Press

The Cabin Crew Interview Made Easy

The Flight Attendant Interview Just Got Even Easier...

The ultimate edition by Caitlyn Rogers

ISBN: 978 0 9560735 4 9

First Edition Published by CE Publishing 2006 (978 0 9552818 3 9)
Second Edition Published by Aspire Publishing 2009 (978 0 9552818 1 8)

Published by Aspire Press
www.aspire-enterprises.co.uk
publishing@aspire-enterprises.co.uk

A CIP catalogue record for this book can be obtained from the British library

Printed in the United Kingdom
10 9 8 7 6 5 4 3

This book is available at quantity discounts for bulk purchases. Please visit www.aspirepress.co.uk for further information

Praise
For the Book...

Claire Sampson – Customer Review

"Seriously, this book is so jam-packed with practical tips and advice that you will be brimming with confidence and therfore won't need to limit your choice to a small airline simply because it has a more relaxed selection process or less competition.

I would highly recommend this book to anyone looking to get into this exciting career, and any other customer service career for that matter. It is a great reference to have at your side and will not end up being a door stop - I can assure you."

Claudia Mello – Customer Review

"I'd Like to say thank you for the precious book and all the important information you gave everytime I wrote you. I'm so happy because they called from Aspire Airlines telling me I was approved to work for them. I'm going to Dubai in January. Thank you once more."

Angeles Taylor – Customer Review

"After so many years of constant failures, my confidence had been severely battered and I was attending interviews expecting to fail. Things changed when I found this guide by Caitlyn Rogers. Her guide gave me the much needed confidence boost I was lacking by providing me with techniques and advice that I could apply throughout each stage of the interview process. The next interview I attended, I felt confident, rejuvenated and most important of all, I felt prepared. As a result, I am now in training with one of the UK's top airlines."

Disclaimer...

This book is designed to provide information and guidance on attending a cabin crew assessment. It is sold with the understanding that the publisher and author are not engaged in rendering legal or other professional services. Such topics, as discussed herein are, for example, or illustrative purposes only. If expert assistance is required, the services of a competent professional should be sought where you can explore the unique aspects of your situation and can receive specific advice tailored to your circumstances.

It is not the purpose of this guide to reprint all the information that is otherwise available to candidates but instead to complement, amplify and supplement other texts. You are urged to read all the available material, learn as much as possible about the role and interview techniques and tailor the information to your individual needs.

Every effort has been made to make this guide as complete and accurate as possible. However, this guide contains information that is current only up to the printing date. Interview processes are frequently updated and are often subject to differing interpretations. Therefore, there are no absolutes and this text should be used only as a general guide and not as the ultimate source of information.

All information in this book is offered as an opinion of the author and should be taken as such and used with discretion by the reader. You are solely responsible for your use of this book. Neither the publisher nor the author explicitly or implicitly promises that readers will find employment because of anything written or implied here.

The purpose of this guide is to educate and inform. The author and Aspire Press shall have neither liability nor responsibility to you or anyone else because of any information contained in or left out of this book.

This page has been intentionally left blank

Contents
At a Glance...

Table
Of Contents

3

The Telephone Screening Stage (49)

4

Pre-Interview Preparation (57)

5

Create a Positive Impression (61)

6

The Group Stage (67)

7

The Assessment Stage (77)

10 The Closing Stage (243)

11 Post-Interview (247)

12 The Other Side of the Desk (257)

Preliminary Essentials

Part 1

The Position

The Duties

On the surface, it would appear that airline cabin crew are nothing more than waiters who jet around the world, stay in luxury hotels and get paid, fairly well, for the privilege. The reality of the job, however, is much more complex.

On-board an aircraft, paramedics, police and firefighters aren't just a phone-call away, thus the cabin crew is responsible for taking on these roles. When things go wrong, whether there is a medical emergency, a fire break-out, a terrorism threat, a violent passenger or mechanical failure, the cabin crew is there to take action. This may involve directing passengers during an evacuation, controlling a drunken passenger or administering first aid.

Fortunately, emergency situations aren't an everyday occurrence and, between boarding and disembarkment, crew will generally spend most of their time tending to passenger comfort. While meal and beverage services play a large part of a crew's duties, their responsibilities will be as diverse as the needs of the passengers, and they generally spend much of the flight on their feet tending to those needs.

All the while, they are expected to deliver the highest standards of customer care, appearing friendly and approachable to every passenger. As if all that wasn't enough, they must also remain calm and professional in all circumstances, regardless of the conditions.

And, a cabin crew's job doesn't just begin and end with the boarding and disembarkement of a flight. Behind the scenes, there is also the cleaning and preparation of the aircraft between flights, the completion of paperwork, stock checks and replenishment, and safety procedures to complete.

Clearly, the profession is a very demanding one, but it is also a very exciting and fulfilling one for those who have the necessary qualities and are willing to put in the effort.

So, in a nutshell, here is a brief recap of the typical duties...

- Cleaning & maintenance of cabins and galleys
- Stock check & replenishment
- Testing of emergency equipment
- Overseeing the boarding and disembarkment of passengers
- Assisting passengers with their luggage
- Providing meal and beverage services
- Overseeing duty-free sales
- Completing paperwork of on-board sales and safety checks
- Advising of safety procedures and carrying out safety demonstrations
- Dealing with problems or issues that arise during the flight
- Taking charge during adverse and emergency situations

The Lifestyle

Working as a cabin crew member provides a very stimulating lifestyle where no two working days are likely to be the same. The sheer dynamics of different crew, passenger profiles, destinations and roster structures ensure that there will always be variety.

Furthermore, there are opportunities to visit places and experience cultures that are beyond most people's reach. Cabin crew visit destinations they always dreamed of and find interest in places they would not necessarily have chosen to go to. A very appealing lifestyle indeed.

On the flip side, crew members experience flight delays and cancellations just as passengers do. The crew, however, experience these much more frequently and much of their time will be spent waiting around in airports and hotels. This makes for very long and tiring shifts, irregular working patterns and unpredictable schedules, which can be very demanding on your family and social life.

In addition, jet lag may also become a problem when regularly crossing different time zones which can lead to disturbed sleep patterns and fatigue. This combined with working in a confined and pressurized container with lots of time spent on your feet, constantly attending to passengers needs can be the cause of high stress levels.

Ultimately, the role is a very physically and mentally demanding one which shouldn't be taken lightly. The rewards are plenty, but the job is not for the faint of heart or those who crave routine.

Career Advancement Opportunities

Depending on the airline, high performing cabin crew can move through to serve the first class cabins, then onto a senior crew member and potentially a flight purser. There are also opportunities to become cabin crew trainers, or even recruitment personnel.

The Requirements

In making a decision about the employment of cabin crew, all airlines consider three key elements: Eligibility, Suitability and Specific Requirements... Put together these three elements form a 'Person Specification' which the airline uses to determine if a candidate is suitable or not.

Eligibility

Eligibility checks are based on facts that can be determined either by physical or documentary evidence and are likely to include:

- Does the candidate have a passport?
- Does the passport allow the candidate to fly to all the countries the airline operates to?
- Has the candidate passed the airline's in house tests?
- Does the candidate meet the required age profile?
- Does the candidate meet the required height/weight profile?
- Has the candidate attained the required educational qualifications?
- Has the candidate acquired adequate experience in a customer service or public contact role?
- Can the candidate speak fluent English?

Not all airlines are the same, so in order to avoid disappointment candidates are recommended to investigate eligibility criteria carefully before applying.

Suitability

Unlike eligibility which is based on facts, suitability involves identifying the right personal qualities.

To summarize, the minimum requirement is for reliable and presentable individuals, who can interact well with people, provide a service in a friendly way, work as part of a team and cope well under pressure and in adverse conditions.

Specific Airline Requirements

Eligibility and Suitability are basic requirements, which must be met in all cases. Airlines then proceed to customize their requirements according to their own needs and standards.

A good example of this is through the requirements for swimming ability. Some airlines will have a specific distance requirement while others may require candidates have the additional ability to tread water. Some airlines have no swimming requirement at all.

Other examples are for certain language abilities, customer service and/or medical experience.

Some airlines see above average appearance as being crucial, whilst others prefer a higher degree of charisma and personality. A new airline may choose previous cabin crew experience as a prime requisite where as a prestigious and well established airline can often afford to be even more particular and demand a combination of preferred attributes.

Once all the considerations are taken into account, the person specification is complete. These different considerations help to explain why some people are successful with one airline, and yet get rejected by another, their performance is obviously another factor.

It is also true that some candidates fail to be recruited by an airline at one attempt, and then succeed at a later date. This is usually because the candidate has acquired better interview technique or extra skills, experience or confidence. It can also be because the airline itself has revised its person specification.

Weight

Airlines generally require that your weight is in proportion to your height. Don't be put off if you are slightly over or underweight because most airlines aren't overly strict about enforcing the height to weight policy as long as you are within the approximate range.

In order to determine height and weight proportions, it is likely that an airline will refer to the body mass index (BMI). The Body Mass Index (BMI) is a formula used by health professionals to determine an adult's healthy body weight in relation to their height. Following is a BMI chart for you to work out your own proportions.

Note: if the majority of your body mass is made up of muscle, if you are pregnant or lactating, this chart may provide inaccurate results.

Body Mass Index (BMI) Chart for Adults

Obese (>30)   Overweight (25-30)   Normal (18.5-25)   Underweight (<18.5)

HEIGHT in feet/inches and centimeters

WEIGHT lbs (kg)	4'8" 142cm	4'9" 147	4'10" 150	4'11" 152	5'0" 155	5'1" 157	5'2" 160	5'3" 163	5'4" 165	5'5" 168	5'6" 170	5'7" 173	5'8" 175	5'9" 178	5'10" 180	5'11" 183	6'0" 185	6'1" 188	6'2" 191	6'3" 193	6'4" 193	6'5" 196
260 (117.9)	58	56	54	53	51	49	48	46	45	43	42	41	40	38	37	36	35	34	33	32	32	31
255 (115.7)	57	55	53	51	50	48	47	45	44	42	41	40	39	38	37	36	35	34	33	32	31	30
250 (113.4)	56	54	52	50	49	47	46	44	43	42	40	39	38	37	36	35	34	33	32	31	30	30
245 (111.1)	55	53	51	49	48	46	45	44	42	41	40	38	37	36	35	34	33	32	31	31	30	29
240 (108.9)	54	52	50	48	47	45	44	43	41	40	39	38	36	35	34	33	33	32	31	30	29	28
235 (106.6)	53	51	49	47	46	44	43	42	40	39	38	37	36	35	34	33	32	31	30	29	29	28
230 (104.3)	52	50	48	46	45	43	42	41	39	38	37	36	35	34	33	32	31	30	30	29	28	27
225 (102.1)	50	49	47	45	44	43	41	40	39	37	36	35	34	33	32	31	31	30	29	28	27	27
220 (99.8)	49	48	46	44	43	42	40	39	38	37	36	34	33	32	32	31	30	29	28	27	27	26
215 (97.5)	48	47	45	43	42	41	39	38	37	36	35	34	33	32	31	30	29	28	28	27	26	25
210 (95.3)	47	45	44	42	41	40	38	37	36	35	34	33	32	31	30	29	28	28	27	26	26	25
205 (93.0)	46	44	43	41	40	39	37	36	35	34	33	32	31	30	29	29	28	27	26	26	25	24
200 (90.7)	45	43	42	40	39	38	37	35	34	33	32	31	30	29	28	27	26	26	25	25	24	24
195 (88.5)	44	42	41	39	38	37	36	35	33	32	31	31	30	29	28	27	26	25	25	24	24	23
190 (86.2)	43	41	40	38	37	36	35	34	33	32	31	30	29	28	27	26	26	25	24	24	23	23
185 (83.9)	41	40	39	37	36	35	34	33	32	31	30	29	28	27	26	25	25	24	24	23	23	22
180 (81.6)	40	39	38	36	35	34	33	32	31	30	29	28	27	27	26	25	24	24	23	22	22	21
175 (79.4)	39	38	37	35	34	33	32	31	30	29	28	27	27	26	25	24	24	23	22	22	21	21
170 (77.1)	38	37	36	34	33	32	31	30	29	28	27	27	26	25	24	24	23	22	22	21	21	20
165 (74.8)	37	36	34	33	32	31	30	29	28	27	27	26	25	24	24	23	22	22	21	21	20	20
160 (72.6)	36	35	33	32	31	30	29	28	27	27	26	25	24	24	23	22	22	21	21	20	19	19
155 (70.3)	35	34	32	31	30	29	28	27	27	26	25	24	24	23	22	22	21	20	20	19	19	18
150 (68.0)	34	32	31	30	29	28	27	27	26	25	24	24	23	22	22	21	20	20	19	19	18	18
145 (65.8)	33	31	30	29	28	27	26	25	25	24	23	23	22	21	21	20	19	19	18	18	18	17
140 (63.5)	31	30	29	28	27	26	26	25	24	23	23	22	21	21	20	20	19	18	18	17	17	17
135 (61.2)	30	29	28	27	26	26	25	24	23	22	22	21	21	20	19	19	18	18	17	17	16	16
130 (59.0)	29	28	27	26	25	24	23	22	22	21	20	20	19	19	18	18	17	17	16	16	15	15
125 (56.7)	28	27	26	25	24	24	23	22	21	21	20	20	19	18	18	17	17	16	16	15	15	15
120 (54.4)	27	26	25	24	23	23	22	21	21	20	19	19	18	18	17	17	16	16	15	15	15	14
115 (52.2)	26	25	24	23	22	22	21	20	20	19	19	18	17	17	16	16	16	15	15	14	14	14
110 (49.9)	25	24	23	22	21	21	20	19	19	18	18	17	17	16	16	15	15	14	14	13	13	13
105 (47.6)	24	23	22	21	21	20	19	19	18	17	17	16	16	16	15	15	14	14	13	13	13	12
100 (45.4)	22	22	21	20	20	19	18	18	17	17	16	16	15	15	14	14	14	13	13	12	12	12
95 (43.1)	21	21	20	19	19	18	17	17	16	16	15	15	14	14	14	13	13	13	12	12	12	11
90 (40.8)	20	19	19	18	18	17	16	16	15	15	14	14	13	13	13	12	12	12	11	11	11	11
85 (38.6)	19	18	18	17	17	16	16	15	15	14	14	13	13	13	12	12	12	11	11	11	10	10
80 (36.3)	18	17	17	16	16	15	15	14	14	13	13	13	12	12	11	11	11	11	10	10	10	9

Note: BMI values rounded to the nearest whole number. BMI categories based on CDC (Centers for Disease Control and Prevention) criteria. www.vertex42.com   BMI = Weight[kg] / (Height[m] x Height[m]) = 703 x Weight[lb] / (Height[in] x Height[in])   © 2009 Vertex42 LLC

Figure 1: Body Mass Index (BMI) Chart created by Vertex42.com

Height

Airlines have strict minimum and maximum height restrictions. Height restrictions apply because a very short person may have difficulties reaching the overhead compartments. Conversely, a very tall person may find the environment too cramped.

Airlines can be very strict when it comes to height requirements so you must ensure that you meet those requirements. It is possible that the recruiters will take your measurements at some stage during the selection process. Incorrect measurements could result in your interview being terminated.

The height restrictions vary from airline to airline, however, a typical minimum height is 5'2'' (158 cms) and a maximum of 6'2'' (188 cms).

If the airline doesn't have a minimum height, they may have a reach requirement instead. The reach requirement is usually 6'10" (212cm).

Health & Fitness

As cabin crew, you will be in regular contact with and share a pressurized cabin with lots of people. You will fly through different time zones and experience frequent, and possibly dramatic, climatic changes. A strong immune system is vital in coping with these conditions.

A good overall fitness level is also required for dealing with the general physical nature of the job, such as opening heavy emergency doors and standing for long periods.

Officially, the Civil Aviation Authority (CAA) has outlined the following health guidelines for cabin crew:

- Free from any physical or mental illness which might lead to incapacitation or inability to perform cabin crew duties
- Normal cardiorespiratory function
- Normal central nervous system
- Adequate visual acuity 6/9 with or without glasses
- Adequate hearing
- Normal function of ear, nose and throat

The Airline

Preliminary Research

Taking the time to research an airline you want to work for will not only enable you to ask intelligent questions, you will also be able to answer any that are posed. Your informed knowledge will give a positive impression about you and your motivation to work for the airline, thus giving you a competitive edge over less informed candidates.

If you know nothing about the airline other than the colour of the uniform, the salary and their best destinations, you won't be creating a positive impression.

You don't need to know the whole history of the airline, but you should at least know some basic facts.

Read through some of the airlines' literature. Their website is a good place to start.

Salary & Benefits

Salaries for cabin crew vary greatly depending on the airline you are applying to, so you will need to check this yourself before you apply.

You can expect to recieve a set starting salary, plus an hourly flight pay and an overseas allowance.

Other benefits may include:

Please note that not all these benefits will be awarded and should be used as guidance only.

- Relocation
- Free or discounted shared accommodation
- Free duty transport
- Pay increments (awarded accordingly based on individual performance and merit)

- An annual ticket providing return travel to your home country (if the position involves relocation).
- Yearly holiday leave
- Concessional Air Travel privileges for yourself and members of your family (usually available after 6 months service)
- Annual cargo concessions
- Paid maternity and sick leave
- Medical & dental insurance and treatment
- Personal accident insurance worldwide for death or disablement.
- Personal effects insurance scheme whilst employees are travelling anywhere in the world on duty.
- End-of-service benefits
- Utilities Allowance to assist in the payment of rent, water, electricity, etc.
- Telephone Allowance to assist with phone rentals.
- Domestic Help Allowance for eligible employees to assist with home cleaning, etc.

The Application Stage

Part 2

Selection to be interviewed can be very competitive and due to the lengthy waiting period between re-applications, it is crucial that you apply only when you are fully prepared and meet all the minimum requirements.

There are several ways you can register your interest, however, you will want to check the preferred method of application with each airline before proceeding with any one method.

The advancement of technology means that many airlines have moved onto, and prefer, online application facilities. If you don't have easy access to the internet, however, you can request a postal application pack or submit a cover letter and résumé to the airline's recruitment office for consideration.

Note: If you have previously applied and been unsuccessful through the initial screening process, most airlines have a six to twelve month waiting periof between re-applications.

Documents

The Cover Letter

If you are applying via sending your résumé, then the cover letter is a big chance to sell yourself. If you don't sell yourself in the cover letter, the person receiving your application may not get to read your résumé - you must give them a reason to continue reading.

Try to stick to one page so that reading it doesn't seem like a large task and try to leave plenty of white border so that it doesn't appear overloaded.

Begin by explaining your reason for contacting the airline and state that you have enclosed your résumé and photographs for consideration.

You can then go on to explain a little bit about yourself, your experience, what you have to offer and why you are seeking to become cabin crew with the airline. Be positive and don't let modesty prevent you from mentioning your strengths, and never apologise for lack of experience as this will only draw attention to it.

Finally, close the letter by stating that you welcome the opportunity to meet with them to discuss the opportunity further.

If you know the person's name, sign 'yours sincerely' and if you don't, use 'yours faithfully'.

Finished...

Although you want to give them a reason to continue reading you don't want to show all your winning cards at once. The object is to give them a taste of what's to come whilst leaving you plenty more winning hands for the interview.

The following page displays an effective sample for you to work with.

Jane Doe

16 Any Road • AnyWhere
Any Town • AN8 9SE
United Kingdom
(+44) 04587 875848 • janedoe@anymail.com

Aspire Airline   25th July 2007
Cabin Crew Recruitment
O. BOX 29
London
United Kingdom

Dear sir/madam.

I would like to express my strong interest in the position of cabin crew with Aspire Airline, thus I have enclosed a copy of my résumé and photographs for your consideration.

I currently work as a freelance hairdresser and have worked in client-facing roles for more than 8 years. I am looking for a change in my life direction and feel that a career as cabin crew would give me this.

I am a friendly, approachable person and am able to work on my own initiative and as a team player. I am a people person and would deliver excellent customer service to passengers of all levels. I feel with my personality and experience, I would be a valuable asset to Aspire Airline.

I would welcome the opportunity to meet with you to discuss this position and my background in more detail, and to explore the ways I could contribute to the ongoing success of your airline.

I appreciate your consideration and look forward to hearing from you.

Yours faithfully,

Jane Doe
Encl

Figure 2: Sample Cover Letter

The Curriculum Vitae/Résumé

Note: Different countries may have different requirements and styles for résumés, thus the following information should be used as a guide only.

If you think your résumé adds no value beyond getting you an interview, you are mistaken. Your résumé is a very powerful document because it will influence the nature and direction of the interview. The recruiters have no information about you beyond this piece of paper, thus they will use it to formulate suitable questions. If your résumé is strong, it will focus the recruiter's mind on your good points and your achievements, thus the questioning will be based on information that presents your image strongly. This allows an element of predictability, thus giving you back some control. A very powerful alli, wouldn't you agree?

With such a valuable tool at your disposal, it is important that it represents the best you have to offer. Thus I have created the subsequent guidelines.

Keep it concise
Recruitment personnel do not have the time to work through long résumés. You must communicate clearly and concisely the information that you wish to convey about yourself that will be of relevance to them.

Keep it in order
The order of your résumé is vital. You want the most important information such as personal information, key competencies and strengths and present employment to be on the first page. Hobbies and interests, education and training, whilst also very important, can be entered on subsequent pages.

Use quality plain white or ivory paper
Résumés don't have to look boring, but fancy paper isn't the best way to make yours stand out. Instead of using colour paper, which photocopies badly, and uneccessary, over the top glossy and parchment papers, play with the design to make it more interesting and eye catching.

Make it computer, yet human friendly

Because many airlines are now using automated systems, you should compile a résumé that will be pleasant to the human eye, but also computer friendly.

By computer friendly, I mean buzzwords. Buzzwords are words that are related to the job, such as teamwork and customer care. The computer conducts a search for these buzzwords and then produces an overall score. The score represents your suitability and can determine whether you are invited for an interview.

A human friendly résumé will have clear, legible headings to make the résumé easy to navigate with plenty of white space to appear easier on the eyes.

Before you begin constructing your résumé, you should make sure you have the following to hand for reference:

Personal Information
- Passport
- Contact information (telephone number, email, fax)
- Personal statistics (height, weight)

Education and Training Details
- Names and addresses of institutions
- Qualifications and results
- Dates

Career History
- Names of employers
- Dates
- Reference details - *Make sure that you have the appropriate permissions from the company(ies) you state as your referee(s)*

With this information to hand, we can begin.

Figure 3: Sample Résumé - Page 1

PROFILE

I am a friendly, adaptable and responsible individual seeking a cabin crew position within Aspire Airlines. My friendly and positive nature will enable me to fit right in and compliment your existing team, and I could use the customer care skills I have developed over the course of my career to deliver the standard of service that passengers have come to expect from Aspire Airlines.

I'm confident that my friendly and positive nature will enable me to fit right in and compliment your existing team

EXPERIENCE

Freelance Hairdresser   1ˢᵗ Feb '03 - Present

In addition to the technical side of being a stylist, I run all aspects of the business, which includes managing and maintaining a client base consisting of over 100 clients. Customer satisfaction is vital to the survival of my business and so it is important that I provide a consistently high standard of service and be friendly and professional at all times.

Any Hair Salon | Senior Stylist   16ᵗʰ Aug '00 – 1ˢᵗ Feb '03

In addition to the technical aspects of being a stylist, I was responsible for consulting with clients and providing advice. Being in a senior position within the salon, I was also responsible for supervising a team of four junior-level stylists and training of an apprentice. On several occasions, I took on the additional responsibility of hiring and training work experience students.

Any Hair Salon - Junior Stylist   05ᵗʰ April '98 – 16ᵗʰ Aug '00

In addition to the technical aspects of being a stylist, I was responsible for consulting with clients, providing advice and ensuring their comfort and satisfaction.

Any Hair Salon - Receptionist   24ᵗʰ July '96 – 5ᵗʰ April '98

Being the first point of contact into the salon, it was important that I gave a positive impression of the salon as a whole by providing a friendly, yet professional service. I was responsible for welcoming customers into the salon, dealing with their enquiries, as well as ensuring their comfort. In between meets and greets, I would carry out general clerical duties such as diary maintenance, calculating the clients bills and collecting payments, cashing up at close of trading and providing a point of sale for retail goods.

+44 04587 875848
janedoe@anymail.com

16 Any Road
Any Where
Any Town
AN8 9SE
United Kingdom

Jane Doe

Continued From Page 1....

I'm positive that my skills and experience will enable me to make a positive contribution to the airline's ongoing success

EDUCATION

Secondary Education
Any High School 91 – 96

Qualifications
11 GCSE's (grade A–D)

Further Education
Any College 97 - 18
Any College 98 – 99
Any College99 – 01
Any College 01

Awards
NVQ 1 – Hairdressing
NVQ 2 - Hairdressing
NVQ 3 - Hairdressing
Certificate in Creative Cutting

OTHER TRAINING

British Red Cross | Basic First Aid – Sept '06
Any Training Centre | Assertiveness – July '07

LANGUAGES

Fluent in spoken and written English
Basic conversational ability in French

INTERESTS

I have been a keen footballer for as long as I can remember and am an active member of Aspire women's football club where I have been captain of the team for 3 years. I have an active interest in nature and regularly get involved with and manage conservation assignments. To relax, I attend yoga and meditation classes that help to keep me focused and relieve stress.

REFERENCES

+44 04587 875848
janedoe@anymail.com

16 Any Road
Any Where
Any Town
AN8 9SE
United Kingdom

Any Hair Salon

Mrs S. Cook - Supervisor
188 Any Road
Any Town
Any Where
AN8 7DE

Any Beauty Salon

Mrs R. Matthews - Manager
298 Any Road
Any Town
Any Where
AN8 8GH

Figure 4: Sample Résumé - Page 2

The Application Form

The purpose of the application form is to provide selectors with an overview of the applicant. Selectors will use the form to formulate the most appropriate questions to ask at the interview, explore a candidate's motives and screen out unsuitable candidates.

Selection to be interviewed can be extremely competitive and, therefore, you need to market yourself well by keeping as closely as possible to the following guidelines.

Don't leave blanks
If a question doesn't apply to you, simply state 'Not Applicable' or 'N/A'.

Don't volunteer negative information
Providing negative information will only provide reasons for the airline not to interview you. Keep your information positive.

Keep it neat
Try to keep your answers within the spaces provided. It is highly recommended that you complete the form in pencil first so that any adjustments can be easily made.

Keep it free from errors
To create a professional impression, you need to ensure your answers are free from typos, scribbles and inaccuracies.

Use black ink
Once you have proofread your answers and are satisfied that no errors exist, you are ready to finish the form in ink. Black ink is usually preferred and is, therefore, recommended.

Use BLOCK CAPITALS
Block capitals is generally preferred due to readability and tidiness.

Consider the example in figure 4. The first example sticks to the above guidelines which creates an overall positive impression of the candidate. Meanwhile, the second example is messy, full of typos and barely legible. It is clear that the candidate jumped straight in without planning. Hardly a positive first impression. Who would you invite to attend an interview?

Figure 5: Application Form Do's and Don'ts

I CURRENTLY WORK AS A FREELANCE HAIRDRESSER AND HAVE WORKED IN CLIENT-FACING ROLES FOR MORE THAN 8 YEARS. I AM LOOKING FOR A CHANGE IN MY LIFE DIRECTION AND FEEL THAT A CAREER AS CABIN CREW WILL GIVE ME THIS. I AM A PEOPLE PERSON AND WOULD DELIVER EXCELLENT CUSTOMER SERVICE TO PASSENGERS OF ALL LEVELS. I FEEL WITH MY EXPERIENCE, I WOULD BE A VALUABLE ASSET TO ASPIRE AIRLINE.

I curently work as a freelance hairdressser and have worked in client-facing roles more than 8 years. I am looking for a change in my life direction and feel ~~that~~ a career as cabin crew would give me this. I am a people ~~pason~~ person and would deliver excellent customer service to passengers of all levels. I feel with my experience, I would be a valuable asset to Aspire Airline.

Before you begin filling in the application form, you should make sure you have the following to hand for reference:

Personal Information
- Passport
- Contact information (telephone number, email, fax)
- Personal statistics (height, weight)

Education and Training Details
- Names and addresses of institutions
- Qualifications and results
- Dates

Career History
- Names of employers
- Dates
- Reference details - *Make sure that you have the appropriate permissions from the company(ies) you state as your referee(s)*

With this information to hand, we can begin.

The following pages present a sample completed application for guidance. Due to the self explanatory nature of the majority of questions, only those that require additional guidance will be elaborated on further.

FOR OFFICE USE ONLY:
Reference: ☐   Interview Base: ☐

Aspire Airlines

Application for Cabin Crew Employment
(Please answer all questions. Where not applicable, please indicate N/A.)

All information supplied will be treated as confidential. Subject to meeting the eligibility criteria you will be invited for our next selection day. Correct information will be a condition of employment.

Full Name (Mr~~Miss~~(Ms))   JANE DOE   Date Available: 29/01/10

Present Address	**Permanent Address** *(if different)*
22 ANY STREET ANY TOWN	N/A

Post code AN2 6DG   Country UNITED KINGDOM   Post code ____   Country ____

Please give telephone number in the format: Country Code + City/Mobile Code + Phone Number

Telephone (Residence): 44 020 374693   Telephone (Residence): ____
Telephone (Mobile): 44 7509 283799   Telephone (Mobile): ____
Email: J.DOE@HOTMAIL.COM

Personal Information

Passport Number: 200654398 76   Expiry date: 09/2011
Date of Birth: 11/09/1979   Gender: ~~Male~~ Female
Marital Status: SINGLE   Nationality: BRITISH

Height (cm): 154   Weight (kg): 49
Do you have any tattoos or body piercings? Yes~~No~~   If yes, please specify. N/A
How would you rate your ability to swim? I cannot swim   Poor   Average ✓ Good   Excellent

---

Education

From	To	Name & Address of School/College	Subject(s)	Results Achieved
09/99	07/01	ANY COLLEGE, ANY WHERE ANY TOWN, AN8 4JN	HAIRDRESSING	NVQ LEVEL 3 - DISTINCTION
09/98	07/99	ANY COLLEGE, ANY WHERE ANY TOWN, AN8 4JN	HAIRDRESSING	NVQ LEVEL 2 - MERIT
09/97	07/98	ANY COLLEGE, ANY WHERE ANY TOWN, AN8 4JN	HAIRDRESSING	NVQ LEVEL 1 - DISTINCTION
09/91	07/96	ANY SCHOOL, ANY WHERE ANY TOWN, AN8 6DT	ENGLISH, MATHS, GEOGRAPHY, FRENCH, CDT, SCIENCE, ART, DESIGN, BUSINESS STUDIES	GCSE - GRADES A-C

Figure 6: Sample Application Form - Page 1

EMPLOYMENT HISTORY

Present/Last Employer

Employer: SELF EMPLOYED

Type of Business: HAIRDRESSING

Address: N/A

From: 01/02/2003 **To:** PRESENT

Position: FREELANCE HAIR CONSULTANT

Notice Required: N/A

Reason for Leaving: TO PURSUE A CAREER AS CABIN CREW

Salary: 15,000

Responsibilities: IN ADDITION TO THE TECHNICAL SIDE OF BEING A STYLIST, I RUN ALL ASPECTS OF THE BUSINESS WHICH INCLUDES MANAGING AND MAINTAINING A CLIENT BASE CONSISTING OF OVER 100 CLIENTS. CUSTOMER SATISFACTION IS VITAL TO THE SURVIVAL OF MY BUSINESS AND SO IT IS IMPORTANT THAT I PROVIDE A CONSISTENTLY HIGH STANDARD OF SERVICE AND BE FRIENDLY AND PROFESSIONAL AT ALL TIMES.

Previous Employment   *Continue on a separate sheet if necessary*

Employer: ANY HAIR SALON

Type of Business: HAIRDRESSING

Address: 159 ANY CITY CENTRE
ANY TOWN, ANY WHERE, AN9 9EF

Reason for Leaving: TO PURSUE freelance OPPORTUNITY

Salary: 12,000

From: 16/08/2000 **To:** 01/02/2003

Position: SENIOR STYLIST

Responsibilities: IN ADDITION TO THE TECHNICAL ASPECTS OF BEING A STYLIST, I WAS RESPONSIBLE FOR CONSULTING WITH CLIENTS AND PROVIDING ADVICE. BEING IN A SENIOR POSITION WITHIN THE SALON, I WAS ALSO RESPONSIBLE FOR SUPERVISING A TEAM OF FOUR JUNIOR-LEVEL STYLISTS AND TRAINING AN APPRENTICE.

Employer: ANY HAIR SALON

Type of Business: HAIRDRESSING

Address: 159 ANY CITY CENTRE
ANY TOWN, ANY WHERE, AN9 9EF

Reason for Leaving: TO PURSUE PROMOTION OPPORTUNITY

Salary: 9000

From: 05/04/1998 **To:** 16/08/2000

Position: JUNIOR STYLIST

Responsibilities: IN ADDITION TO THE TECHNICAL ASPECTS OF BEING A STYLIST, I WAS RESPONSIBLE FOR CONSULTING WITH CLIENTS, PROVIDING ADVICE AND ENSURING THEIR COMFORT AND SATISFACTION.

Employer: ANY HAIR SALON

Type of Business: HAIRDRESSING

Address: 159 ANY CITY CENTRE
ANY TOWN, ANY WHERE, AN9 9EF

Reason for Leaving: TO PURSUE PROMOTION OPPORTUNITY

Salary: 7,000

From: 24/07/1997 **To:** 05/04/1998

Position: RECEPTIONIST

Responsibilities: BEING THE FIRST POINT OF CONTACT INTO THE SALON IT WAS IMPORTANT THAT I GAVE A POSITIVE IMPRESSION OF THE SALON AS A WHOLE BY PROVIDING A FRIENDLY YET PROFESSIONAL SERVICE. I WAS RESPONSIBLE FOR WELCOMING CLIENTS INTO THE SALON, DEALING WITH THEIR ENQUIRIES, AS WELL AS ENSURING THEIR COMFORT. IN BETWEEN MEET AND GREETS, I WOULD CARRY OUT GENERAL CLERICAL DUTIES.

Please explain any gaps of unemployment

UPON LEAVING SCHOOL IN 1996, I SPENT 12 MONTHS TRAVELLING BEFORE EMBARKING ON EMPLOYMENT.

Please list any charity work

FOR THE PAST 3 YEARS I HAVE VOLUNTEERED AT THE LOCAL SAMARITANS HOUSING SHELTER DURING THE CHRISTMAS PERIOD WHERE I HELP COOK AND SERVE BEVERAGES TO THE HOMELESS.

Figure 7: Sample Application Form - Page 2

Additional Training

Give details of any first aid and/or nursing qualifications

BRITISH RED CROSS BASIC FIRST AID CERTIFICATE - 09/2006

Give details of languages spoken and ability

ENGLISH - FLUENT
SPANISH - BASIC CONVERSATIONAL ABILITY

Give details of any other training

I HAVE ATTENDED AND PASSED SHORT COURSES IN LEADERSHIP AND COMMUNICAITON SKILLS, AND COMPUTING.

Hobbies/Outside Interests

I HAVE AN ACTIVE SOCIAL LIFE AND REGULARLY GO SWIMMING, CYCLING AND PLAY TENNIS I AM CAPTAIN OF THE LOCAL FOOTBALL TEAM AND REGULARLY ATTEND SNOOKER TOURNAMENTS NATIONWIDE. I LIKE TO SOCIALISE WITH MY FRIENDS AND WE OFTEN GO DANCING AND BOWLING. I AM AN AVID TRAVELLER AND LOVE THE GREAT OUTDOORS.

Use the following space to provide any further information you feel will benefit your application

BEING A MEMBER OF CABIN CREW HAS ALWAYS BEEN A LIFELONG AMBITION OF MIN AND I HAVE NOW REACHED A STAGE IN MY LIFE WHERE I AM PREPARED TO MAKE THE CAREER AND LIFESTYLE CHANGE.

BEING CABIN CREW, I COULD USE THE CUSTOMER CARE AND TEAMWORKING SKILLS I HAVE DEVELOPED OVER THE COURSE OF MY CAREER TO DELIVER THE STANDARD OF SERVICE THAT PASSENGERS EXPECT, WHILE AT THE SAME TIME, BE SUFFICIENTLY CHALLENGED TO DEVELOP FURTHER WHILE LEARNING FROM NEW PEOPLE AND PROCESSES.

FURTHERMORE, I AM A FRIENDLY, ADAPTABLE AND RESPONSIBLE INDIVIDUAL WHO HAS PROVEN TO BE A HARD WORKER, CAPABLE OF WORKING UNDER PRESSURE. AN ESSENTIAL SKILL THAT WILL TRANSFER WELL AND BENEFIT MY PERFORMANCE AS A CABIN CREW MEMBER WITH ASPIRE AIRLINES.

Declaration

Have you been convicted of any offence which, at the date of the application, is not a spent conviction as defined in the Rehabilitation of Offenders Act 1974?   YES/NO   *If YES then such conviction(s) must be disclosed below.*

N/A

Have you ever been refused entry, or deported from a foreign country? YES/NO *If YES please provide details*

N/A

The details given on this application are correct to my knowledge and belief. I understand that my application may be rejected or that I may be dismissed for withholding relevant details or giving false information. I am aware that my employment with Aspire Airlines will be subject to satisfactory references, medical form and criminal record checks.

Signature   Date   5/1/2010

Figure 8: Sample Application Form - Page 3

Notes on Completion

Employment history
How much history you provide is based entirely on your preference and circumstance.

Most employers are only interested in your more recent experience, say five years or so. However, if you have gained highly relevant experience beyond five years or feel your history demonstrates your dedication, a solid career path or promotional growth, a full historical account may well work to your advantage.

On the other hand, if your history is very fragmented or you were fired from a position, drawing unnecessary attention will not do you any favours and is best left undocumented.

Lack of relative experience
If you lack experience, you should definately get some. Whether you take on a short term voluntary post at a local charity shop or some weekend bar work, anything will add bulk and strengthen your application. There are lots of opportunities available for those who are willing.

Gaps in employment
If you have gaps in your employment history, you may be asked to elaborate on these. Whatever your reasons, maternity leave, study break or travel break, be honest and positive, and be prepared to discuss the details openly at interview.

If you were doing anything during the gaps, paid or unpaid, it would be best to insert them into your work history to fill the hole.

For example: 2005 – 2009 - Full Time Parent
                Summer 2004 – Winter 2004 – Traveled around Europe

Career progression
If you have remained with an employer for several years, but have moved up through the ranks, you will want to list your progression within the company as though you were listing a new job. This will make your progression more obvious.

Fragmented work history

A fragmented job history, one that is made up of lots of short-term jobs, will give the impression of a job hopper, not a favourable impression to a potential employer. To avoid being viewed negatively, there are several things you can do:

- Where several consecutive jobs appear that are similar in nature, you can combine them into one chunk.

Eg:	2004 – 2006	Receptionist
		Aspire Hotel & Spa, Aspire Leisure Centre, Aspire Hair Salon
	2007 – 2008	Waiter
		Aspire Restaurant & Bar, Aspire Take Away

- Don't draw attention to the dates by having them as headers on your résumé. Put the dates at the end of the descriptions and leave off the months if you feel you are able.
- If a job was very brief and didn't provide any essential experience, you can drop it altogether.
- Instead of listing specific dates for summer jobs, you can simply state Summer 20xx to Spring 20xx.

Responsibilities

In order to communicate your suitability for the position clearly, you must highlight the relevant skills and experience you have gained within each role.

For example, a receptionist may include the following:

'Being the first point of contact into the salon, it was important that I gave a positive impression of the salon as a whole by providing a friendly, yet professional service. I was responsible for welcoming customers into the salon, dealing with their enquiries, as well as ensuring their comfort.

In between meets and greets, I would carry out general clerical duties such as diary maintenance, calculating the clients bills and collecting payments, cashing up at close of trading and providing a point of sale for retail goods.'

A customer complaint handler, on the other hand, might use this statement:

'Working in a busy call centre, my job involved delivering the highest level of customer service whilst investigating and resolving queries and complaints. This involved following procedure to ensure that each case was resolved efficiently and professionally to a mutually agreeable conclusion.

Being a constant target for customers to vent their frustration on, it was important that I remained calm, diplomatic and professional at all times in order to maintain customer satisfaction.'

Both statements highlight extensive customer contact experience as well as other specific responsibilities and attributes that are required of cabin crew. It would be clear to any airline that both these candidates have the necessary experience and are clearly suited for the position.

Reasons for leaving

Your reasons for leaving your current employment will likely involve your passion to pursue a career as cabin crew. You will want to state this and expand if space permits.

Your reasons for leaving your previous employment may be for any reason – career advancement, not enough hours, wider responsibilities, temporary contract, redundancy, maternity leave, study break, travel break, company relocation, etc... Whatever your reason, you should keep the wording positive by avoiding phrases such as fired, terminated, quit, illness and personal reasons, These resonses create negative impressions and will reduce your chances.

If you were fired, use neutral words such as 'involuntary separation'. If you quit under less than favourable conditions, avoid being negative about your past employer and use terms such as 'voluntary separation'. Alternatively, in any case, you can simply state 'Will explain at the interview' or 'job ended'. Both of these will provide you with the opportunity to discuss the details openly at interview where you can create a more favourable and detailed response.

Remember, you should not lie about your reasons for leaving previous employment posts.

Additional training/activities

Additional self improvement attempts, such as educational achievements and volunteer work, give a favourable impression about your character, your work ethics and your ambition.

Self-appraisal/Personal profile

Within an application form, a self appraisal can appear in many forms. A common example would be: "State your reason for applying and why you feel you are suited to the position of cabin crew" or simply, "Please provide any further information you feel will benefit your application"

On your résumé, the self appraisal will be in the form of a personal profile.

Essentially, this is an opportunity to sell yourself, and you should, therefore, provide a power statement which summarises your experience, highlights your key skills and shares your motives all within a few short sentences.

Consider the following example:

"I am a friendly, adaptable and responsible individual seeking a cabin crew position within Aspire Airlines. My friendly and positive nature will enable me to fit right in and compliment your existing team, and I could use the customer care skills I have developed over the course of my career to deliver the standard of service that passengers have come to expect from Aspire Airlines."

The above example is concise, it focuses on what you can offer the airline rather than what the airline can offer you, and it showcases skills and experiences that are an asset for a cabin crew position. This example would work well as a personal profile.

Here's another example, this time more suited to the application form.

"Because this job is tailored to my core competencies, which includes excellent people skills and the ability to remain calm under pressure, I am confident that I am perfect for the position of cabin crew.

My friendly and positive nature will enable me to fit right in and compliment your existing team, and I could use the customer care skills I have developed over the course of my career to deliver the standard of service that passengers have come to expect from Aspire Airlines.

I feel that, for the above reasons, I would be successful as cabin crew and would make a positive contribution to the position, and the airline."

Leisure interests
Personal interests reveal a great deal about your character. You should, therefore, use this section to support and strengthen your application. This can be achieved by making your answer specific and interesting, thus humanizing and creating depth to your character.

Generalised list statements such as 'reading, watching television, sport and socialising' are not only bland, they are also too common which won't make you stand out. Likewise, there is no need to list everything that interests you in an attempt to appear more rounded and interesting. Instead, you should limit your selection to just three or four and achieve balance by listing a mix of individual pursuits and group activities.

Don't be tempted to just tell them what you think they want to hear. Exaggerations or untruths can come back to haunt you if you're are quizzed about them at the interview.

Your leisure pursuits can be good ice-breakers and can provide further evidence of business skills such as team-working and managerial ability. This can be advantageous if you lack certain skills or experience.

Avoid: 'I enjoy spending time with my mates, hitting the town and going out on the razz. I love to shop as I find it very relaxing.'

This individuals' statement lacks variety and doesn't highlight any key skills. Worse still is their choice of wording, which sounds very unprofessional, not something you would expect to see on a formal application form. This statement would highlight some serious potential concerns to an employer which would quite literally knock them out of contention.

Use: 'I have been a keen footballer for as long as I can remember and am an active member of Aspire women's football club where I have been captain of the team for 3 years. I have an active interest in nature and regularly get involved with and manage conservation assignments. To relax, I attend yoga and meditation classes, which help to keep me focused and relieve stress.'

This individual's statement gives an impression of balance. Their interests highlight several admirable qualities such as commitment, team-working and managerial skills as well as their methods of stress management. A recruitment office would form a positive impression of the candidate based on a statement such as this.

References

Always get permission from the person(s) you state as your referee(s) and give them a copy of your application form or résumé to help them write a relevant reference that highlights your most important points.

If you don't have any work references that you can use, either through lack of work experience, maybe your previous supervisor has moved on or your employment with a particular company was too long ago, you should provide a character reference instead. This can be a schoolteacher, university lecturer or a friend in an authoritative position such as a policeman.

If you have been fired, or you resigned under less than favourable circumstances, you may want to call the employer to find out what they would say in response to reference checks. Usually, past employers will agree to use the term 'resigned' if you explain that your termination is hurting your chances of finding employment.

The Photographs

With so many applications being submitted to airlines for cabin crew positions, it would be virtually impossible to keep track of candidates without a visual reminder that recruiters can refer back to.

Airlines will, therefore, request each candidate to provide a head and shoulder shot, normally in the form of a passport photo. For some airlines this will be sufficient, while others may require an accompanying full length shot.

Your photographs will be the only thing the recruiters see before meeting you in person, and it will be the last thing they see before making any hiring decisions. It is, therefore, vital that you present yourself well to give yourself the best possible chance.

Although the airline will advise you of their specific requirements when you apply, the following pages will provide guidance that will assist you in creating a positive first and last impression.

Figure 9: Sample Passport Photographs

Figure 10: Sample Full Length Photograph – Female

Figure 11: Sample Full Length Photograph – Male

Professional vs. Casual

The requirements for candidate photographs vary from airline to airline. While some airlines may be content to receive casual snaps, others may not even invite you to attend an interview with anything less than professional shots. For this reason, I recommend you always opt for the latter. Let's face it, you can never go wrong with a professional image.

Attire

As cabin crew, you will be the face of the airline and your standards of presentation should, therefore, be very high. Smart, business attire will give the appearance of professionalism, as well as the impression of cabin crew material.

Female candidates are highly recommended to wear a skirt, rather than trousers as they create a more feminine and streamlined appearance.

Ensure your attire is clean and crisp, and your shoes are well polished with no obvious scuffed or tatty edges.

And finally, don't be afraid to introduce colour into your outfit, a brightly coloured blouse or unique tie can give you character and make you stand out.

Background

A solid background will give a clean, uncluttered appearance, thus producing the best results.

If your attire is white or cream, you should go for a contrasting background colour such as pale blue, otherwise a white background is ideal.

A hanging bed sheet will not look professional, so don't do it.

Appearance

To provide a polished look you should make use of cosmetics. Concentrate particularly on covering any blemishes as well as emphasizing your cheeks, lips and eyes. Don't go over the top, instead try to retain a natural look.

Your hair should be neat and well groomed. Outrageous colours or styles should be avoided.

Male cabin crew are not normally permitted to have beards so it is recommended that you are cleanly shaven. If you must have facial hair, it must be closely trimmed.

Hands & Nails
Ensure that your nails are tidy and not too long. Nail polish should be conservative and match in colour. Avoid charms, glitter and multi-coloured polish.

Tattoos & Jewellery
Visible tattoos and facial piercings are not acceptable. Tattoos will need to be concealed and piercings removed.

Jewellery should be minimal and conservative. Wear no more than one ring per hand. Avoid cloth or rope bracelets and thumb rings.

Smile
A friendly and welcoming smile will complete the look.

What Happens Next?

Those who are successful at the application stage are usually contacted within six weeks of the application close-off date and invited to attend a preliminary selection process.

In the unfortunate case that you have been unsuccessful, most airlines will require a minimum six month waiting period between re-applications. You will need to check each airline's requirement.

The Telephone Screening Stage

Part 3

Not all airlines will have a telephone screening system in place, however, if it does arise, I have prepared the following guidelines to give you the best chance of success.

What to Expect

Telephone screenings vary from airline to airline and generally come in two forms:

The first type, general screening, is usually quite straightforward and consists of a series of simple questions, which seek to identify your eligibility, such as: 'Are you over 5'2" tall?', 'Are you over xx years old?', 'Do you have customer service experience?' and so forth.

The second type is more comparable to an interview than it is a screening. It is much more in depth, and you can expect tougher elimination questions, such as: 'Why do you want to work for us?' 'Why do you want to be cabin crew?' And 'What is your greatest weakness?'

Both types of screening allow an airline to determine if a candidate meets the eligibility criteria, thus eliminating unlikely candidates without going to the expense of inviting them to attend an interview. The information you supply at this stage is vital to your continuation in the process so you need to be prepared.

Be Prepared

Prepare for potential questions
At the minimum, you should be prepared to answer some basic questions, such as:

- Can you tell me about yourself and your work history?
- Why do you want to work for us?
- What interests you about this job?
- What skills can you bring to the position?

You should also be ready to provide specific examples of accomplishments and experiences which showcase your customer service and teamwork skills.

Setup Voicemail
Ensure that you have a professional sounding voice mail message which details your name and phone number.

Return the call promptly and be prepared to interview immediately or to leave a message with your full contact information and availability.

Using a mobile phone
Where possible, your first choice of contact should be via a land-line telephone. If a mobile phone is your sole option, make sure you have a strong signal and the phone is fully charged. It may be wise to carry a charging cable with you as a backu

Make use of your résumé
To ensure that you can provide precise answers to the recruiter's questions, you should have your résumé in front of you.

Keep a pen and notepad nearby
Write down brief notes about the call, including the callers name and phone number.

If you are offered to attend a formal interview, make a note of the date and time, the location and phone number, and directions to the venue (if offered).

Have a glass of water available
Depending on the length of the conversation and how nervous you become, a dry mouth and throat can become a hazard. For this reason, I would suggest sipping on a glass of water throughout the telephone call.

Make a Positive Impression

Use the recruitment officer's name
Write down the recruiter's name and use it. Unless invited to do so, you shouldn't use their first name, but instead use Mr. or Ms.

Dress the part
Although you won't be personally with the recruitment officer, you should still make an effort to dress appropriately. This doesn't necessarily mean full business attire, but it does mean something that will make you feel relaxed, yet alert and businesslike. Slacks or a bathrobe will hardly make you feel professional, and it certainly won't put you in the correct frame of mind for a formal telephone conversation.

Keep an upright posture
A slouched posture will inhibit your breathing, thus your voice will appear weak and shallow. To give your voice more energy and projection power, try maintaining a good upright posture.

Smile
Your tone of voice is largely related to your facial expression. A frown will give your voice a harsh tone, while a smile will add warmth making it sound friendly, inviting and enthusiastic.

To give yourself a boost, there are several things you can do:

- Keep a humorous, inspirational or special picture nearby
- To remind yourself to smile, keep a mirror in front of you
- Think about someone you care about
- Have a funny joke pinned up
- Have some happy music playing in the background – make sure it is appropriate music though and not too loud

Pay attention to your tone

Because you don't have the benefit of body language and eye contact to express your enthusiasm, you should pay particular attention to the tone of your voice because it plays a key role in sending the correct messages.

If your tone sounds bored and distracted, it won't matter how enthusiastically you phrase your answers because your tone will be the message that sticks with the recruiter. The key is to match the sound of your voice to the words you are using.

To check the level of enthusiasm in your voice, you can practice with a tape recorder.

Be an active listener

Although you should never interrupt the recruiter, this doesn't mean listening in total silence. Instead, you should use active listening, which involves giving feedback via verbal cues. This feedback indicates to the speaker that you are listening, and that you understand, thus the caller will feel encouraged to continue.

Some verbal feedback signals include:

- "uh huh"
- "I see."
- "Yeah"
- "Ok"
- "I understand"

- "That's interesting"
- "Sure"
- "Right"
- "Of course"

Ask for clarification

If you are unsure, or feel you have misunderstood a question, it is better to request the recruiter to repeat, rephrase or summarise the question than to answer the question incorrectly.

Rather than jump straight in with your question, though, you should consider using a polite introductory phrase, such as:

- I beg your pardon but I don't quite follow/understand. I wonder if you could rephrase that in a different way?
- Do you think you could repeat the part about...once again please?
- Pardon me. Would you mind repeating that?
- Sorry, but I'm not sure I'm following you.
- Let's see if I understand/understood you correctly. ...
- Do you/Does this mean then that...
- Would it be correct to say that...
- So in other words...

Speak clearly

You should make a conscious effort to slow the pace of your speech and enunciate clearly. Speaking too fast, too close to the mouthpiece or mumbling will make you harder to understand and definitely hurt your chances.

Give short answers

It is easy to talk too much when you are nervous. To make sure you don't make this mistake, only talk long enough to answer the question. A moment of silence, while it might seem awkward to you, lets the recruiter know that you are done.

Mistakes to Avoid

Trying to lead or control

Don't try to lead or control the conversation, this is the recruitment officer's Job. You can, however, ask questions of your own when opportunities arise.

Distractions & Interruptions

Background noise such as loud music, children screaming and washing machines, are not only distracting, they are also unprofessional.

To minimize potential distractions, take the call in a quiet room and be sure to discourage interruptions from others.

If the recruitment officer does catch you at an inopportune time, politely ask them to hold for a brief moment while you move to a quiet location. You could say "Could you give me a moment to go to a room where we won't be interrupted?" or "Could you give me just a moment to close the door?"

Alternatively, if the timing is a really bad one, you can respectfully request an alternative date and time by saying "I do apologise, but is there a time I can reach you later? I'm very interested in the position and want to give you my undivided attention, but I'm afraid that now isn't the best time.'

Interrupting the recruiter
Unless absolutely necessary, you should never interrupt the recruiter while they are speaking. Write down any questions or comments you have for later.

Unprepared or unnecessary questions
To stand out as an informed and competent applicant, your questions should reflect that you have researched the airline and the position. Asking questions that have already been addressed within the airline's literature will make you appear unprepared and incompetent.

Likewise, asking questions that are based on money and benefits will make you appear selfishly motivated and give a negative impression about your motives for the position and/or the airline.

Being negative
There is no room for negativity when it comes to interviews of any kind. Be especially careful about being negative about other jobs, airlines, people, previous employers and your current job.

Unclear speech
You should make a conscious effort to slow the pace of your speech and enunciate clearly. Speaking too fast, too close to the mouthpiece or mumbling will make you harder to understand and definitely hurt your chances.

Silence

The recruiter cannot see you nod, and may interpret your silence as a dropped line, lack of interest or lack of understanding. Be sure to use occasional active listening cues.

Some verbal feedback signals include:

- "uh huh"
- "I see."
- "Yeah"
- "Ok"
- "I understand"

- "That's interesting"
- "Sure"
- "Right"
- "Of course"

Smoking, chewing or slurping

Any sounds you make close to the receiver will be amplified at the other end so avoid smoking, eating and drinking close to the mouthpiece.

Verbal ticks

Anyways, you know how when you are, like, really nervous, and you ,ummm, find it hard to verbalise and stuff and you say silly things that, kind of, make you sound, like, kind of, unprofessional and maybe, like, inarticulate?

The useless and annoying verbal mannerisms used in the above example "you know," "like," "in other words," "kind of," "ummm," and "anyways." should be avoided at all costs. Besides making you sound unprofessional, they also distract attention from your message.

Making a Successful Close

As the recruitment officer begins to conclude the interview thank them for his or her time and, if they haven't suggested an in person interview, enquire about the next steps and tell them that you are available for a face-to-face interview.

For example, you may say, "I've really enjoyed talking to you and am very interested in the position. What are the next steps in the hiring process? Should I expect to hear from you soon?"

Pre
Interview
Preparation

Part 4

The success of an interview doesn't rely solely on your performance, but also how well prepared you are. If you are well prepared, you will be better organised and feel calmer, thus you will present yourself in a confident and professional manner.

Last Minute Preparation

24 hours is more than enough time to prepare if you break the process down and concentrate on preparing the essential segments first, these are:

1. Prepare for potential questions
At the minimum, you should be prepared to answer some basic questions, such as:

- Can you tell me about yourself and your work history?
- Why do you want to work for us?
- What interests you about this job?
- What skills can you bring to the position?

You should also be ready to provide specific examples of accomplishments and experiences which showcase your customer service and teamwork skills.

2. Learn about the airline
An informed knowledge will give a positive impression about you and your motivation to work for the airline, thus giving you a competitive edge over less informed candidates.

3. Prepare to make a positive first impression
Pick and outfit in advance and get an early night. You will want to arrive at the interview fresh and alert.

4. Draw up a list of questions to ask
The questions you ask will reveal a lot about your level of interest in the airline and your preparedness for the interview so have a couple of questions lined u

5. Familiarise yourself with the location
If time permits, you should take the opportunity to visit the location in advance to familiarise yourself with the location, route, parking and time it will take to get there so that you don't find yourself lost or late on the day.

If you are unable to make an advance visit the location, there are many useful resources on the internet that can provide you with detailed route maps, including the distance and time estimations.

6. Travelling arrangements
If traveling by car, make sure the tank has plenty of petrol, and that you have change available for parking meters. If using public transport, check timetables.

With the groundwork in place and if time permits, you can then continue through the remaining sections of the book.

On the Day

Leave with plenty of time to spare
Arriving late to an interview means you immediately start the interview from behind the rest of the candidates. You also risk arriving in a panic. You should, therefore, aim to arrive at least 10 minutes early and allow extra traveling time to account for any unforeseen delays.

It is better to be an hour early than it is to be just a minute late. You can always grab a coffee and go through your notes.

Have a light snack.
You will need energy for the day, and it can be embarrassing and distracting if your stomach is rumbling during an interview.

Briefcase Essentials

Documentation

- Copies of your résumé
- Interview invitation
- A copy of your application form
- Passport
- Certificates
- Reference details

Photographs
You may have already sent these along with your application, but it is always good to have spares. You should take one full length and one or two passport size.

A notepad
If you wish to take notes, a notepad is tidier than lots of pieces of paper that may get lost.

2 pens
Nothing looks more disorganised than if you have to ask someone to borrow a pen. With two pens, you will have a backup if the first runs out of ink or becomes lost. Alternatively, you can lend one to another candidate.

A wristwatch

Returning from your breaks on time is vital, you do not want to be relying on other people or wall clocks to tell you the time.

A pencil and eraser

If you are required to take part in any assessments or complete any forms, you wouldn't want to be handing in your completed form with lots of scribbles over it. These two items will make mistakes easy to rectify.

Cosmetics & Toiletries

Whenever you get a short bathroom break, ensure you touch up your makeup, and freshen up with some hand cream, mouth spray and deodorant. These items will keep you feeling fresh throughout the day and keep you smelling good also.

A bottle of water and a light snack

The interviews can be long and grueling so you will need a light refreshment when you get short break periods.

Create a Positive Impression

Part 5

Body Language

Your body language conveys all sorts of messages and the right body language will convey the message of a well-balanced confident individual, even if you are not. So, practice using positive body language now so that your body will begin to adopt this new language at a subconscious level.

Here are some points to keep in mind...

Gestures

We use open gestures when we are feeling confident and relaxed,, and are being sincere and honest. Therefore, keep your arms unfolded, your legs uncrossed and your palms open.

Hand gestures, used in moderation, can make you seem enthusiastic and committed to your topic so make use of them if you feel they support your words.

Posture

An upright posture that has a slight forward lean toward the recruiter will make you appear interested and alert, yet confident and relaxed.

A posture that is too erect can make you appear rigid and tense. This may give the impression that you feel uncomfortable and nervous. On the other hand, slouching shows dis-interest and boredom, neither of which will create a positive impression.

Eye contact

Regular, strong eye contact will give the impression of someone who is honest and confident.

Where there is more than one recruitment officer, you should maintain eye contact with the person who asks you the question while occasionally engaging eye contact with the second recruiter .

Tip: If direct eye contact is too much, look at the bridge of the nose.

Smile

A genuine and sincere looking smile will put others at ease around you. It will also give the impression that you are someone who is warm, welcoming, happy and confident.

Tip: If you can't fake it, just think about how lucky the recruiters are to be meeting you.

Mirroring

Mirroring is what happens when you have developed a rapport with another person and your body subconsciously, yet subtly, copies the movements and gestures of the other person.

If you are able to use mirroring techniques without being obvious, you will establish a better rapport with the recruiter.

Project calmness

To be perceived as being professional and relaxed, pay attention to and control inadvertent movements and nervous habits that you make, for example, touching our hair and face, biting our nails, tapping our feet and fidgeting.

Your handshake

A handshake that is brief and firm will convey confidence and professionalism. A weak, limp handshake reflect insecurity and low conifdence and should be avoided. Likewise, handshakes that are too strong may indicate aggression and control, not a favourable first impression.

If the recruiter doesn't extend his or her hand first, don't hesitate to make the initiation.

Tip: If you have a problem with sweaty palms, try using talcum powder and keep a hanky close to hand.

Dress to Impress

During the first few minutes of an interview, the recruitment officers make certain judgments about your character and work style based on your attire, demeanor and body language. I have, therefore, put together the following guidelines to help you present a polished, friendly and conservative image.

Note: It's a mistaken belief that airlines only seek cabin crew who look like super-models. They are looking for the whole package... behaviour, body language and necessary skills/qualifications

Attire

A formal occasion such as a cabin crew interview demands nothing less than business attire. A smart, well tailored suit will give the appearance of professionalism.

Female candidates are highly recommended to wear a skirt, rather than trousers as they create a more feminine and streamlined appearance.

Ensure your attire is clean, crisp, tailored and doesn't crease easily. Your shoes should be polished with no obvious scuffed or tatty edges.

And finally, don't be afraid to introduce colour into your outfit, a brightly coloured blouse or unique tie can give you character and make you stand out.

Tights/Stockings

Even in summer months, female candidates should wear tights or stockings in order to create a sophisticated image.

Appearance

To provide a polished look you should make use of cosmetics. Concentrate particularly on covering any blemishes as well as emphasizing your cheeks, lips and eyes. Don't go over the top, instead try to retain a natural look.

Your hair should be neat and well groomed. Outrageous colours or styles should be avoided.

Male cabin crew are not normally permitted to have beards so it is recommended that you are cleanly shaven. If you must have facial hair, it must be closely trimmed.

Hands & Nails

Ensure that your nails are tidy and not too long. Nail polish should be conservative and match in colour. Avoid charms, glitter and multi-coloured polish.

Tattoos & Jewellery

Visible tattoos and facial piercings are not acceptable. Tattoos will need to be concealed and piercings removed.

Jewellery should be minimal and conservative. Wear no more than one ring per hand. Avoid cloth or rope bracelets and thumb rings.

Perfume/Cologne

If you choose to wear perfume/cologne, select a light scent and wear it sparingly.

Smile

A friendly and welcoming smile will complete the look.

Reduce Anxiety

Nervous feelings before an interview are quite legitimate and simply show that you feel very strongly about the position. Most recruiters recognise this and will make allowances during the first few minutes of the interview. A continual display of nervousness, however, is less likely to be excused.

If your nerves are strong enough to affect your clarity of thought and dialogue, you should address them straight away by using some of the following techniques...

Prepare
Anxiety is partly the result of poor preparation.

If you anticipate potential questions, prepare appropriate answers, research the airline and understand the requirements of the job, you will be more mentally prepared. If your mind is prepared, it makes sense that you will feel calmer and more confident in yourself and your ability to handle the interview.

Visualise Success
Visualisation, when practiced regularly, can dramatically enhance your interview skills and provide you with a much needed confidence boost.

This technique is best done in a quiet and comfortable area where you won't be disturbed. Close your eyes, take several deep breaths and count backwards from ten. Feel your body relaxing as you count.

When running through the event in your mind, see yourself confidently answering questions, feeling relaxed when participating in tasks, and having a positive rapport with the other candidates, and the recruiters.

Once you have mastered the visual aspects, you can also incorporate kinesthetic (feelings) and auditory (sounds) aspects into this mental rehearsal, thereby making the experience more memorable and realistic. So, go ahead and get all your senses involved, let yourself get swept up in the moment. Remember, though, you should try to keep it clear and focused.

Repetiion is the key to success with this technique. The more you practice, the better you will get and the more confident you will feel. Then, by the time the event arrives, your subconscious mind will have positive memories to draw from and thus, you will feel more relaxed and in control.

Adjust your perspective

If you think and believe that this is the last interview you'll ever get, or if you fail it will be the end of the world, you aren't in the right frame of mind and need to readjust your perspective.

Maybe you'll get the job, and maybe you won't, but don't allow your desperation or fear to tarnish your mindset. Negative thoughts will only produce negative results.

Practice deep breathing

Deep breathing will steady your rapid heartbeat, strengthen your shallow breathing and provide your brain with vital oxygen, making you more alert.

Deep breathing is best done standing and is achieved by inhaling slowly and deeply through your nose. Try to fill your lungs completely and after the count of three, feel your shoulders relax as you slowly exhale through your mouth.

You should see your stomach move out each time you breathe in, and flatten when you breathe out. Repeat this deep breathing four to five times.

The
Group
Stage

Part 6

Such a highly sought after and competitive career option requires a carefully designed selection process that will sieve out the right individuals. Group assessments are designed to do just that.

The Recruitment Team

Airlines are aware that some applicants will try to conceal their true personalities by putting on an act to impress the recruitment officers. They also know that candidates are much more relaxed and natural around fellow interviewees. So, in an attempt to uncover the genuine personalities of each candidate, some airlines will utilise this trust by placing a team of recruitment officers undercover during their recruitment days.

Within the role of a fellow candidate, these undercover officers can gain the trust of the applicants and examine each of their behaviours closely. This allows for a much more precise method of separating the unsuitable candidates from the rest of the grou

During the day, they will report their findings back to the official recruiters who can then make more informed decisions and better elimination choices.

Identify the undercover officers?
Undercover officers are actors. They come in many shapes and sizes and their pseudo personalities are just as diverse.

They may play the role of a very nervous and shy individual, or they may be brash and arrogant. Either way, the are generally very good at their jobs so there is little chance that you will identify them.

The other purpose of undercover officers
The scope of an undercover officers' job extends far beyond simply uncovering unsuitable candidates. Their job also involves behaving as role models for others to follow, or avoid.

Some will be confident, yet friendly and behave generally as a model candidate would, thereby demonstrating exactly what the airline is looking for.

Those taking on arrogant, shy, or gossiping behaviours are doing so not only to show what is undesirable, but also to test other people's reactions to them. For instance, are you supportive? Do you actively participate in and encourage bad behaviour? Are you assertive? Do you try to encourage positive behaviour? Do you take a neutral stance? Or do you remove yourself completely?

Undercover candidates who demonstrate undesirable behaviour are intended to fail the interview as an example to other candidates. Whatever your feelings about their observations, if you participate in or encourage this behaviour in any way, you will be joining them at the exit.

Creating and maintaining a positive impression
In order to impress the recruitment team, you must always demonstrate a positive attitude by appearing friendly, helpful and supportive of other candidates and being positive about any tasks or tests you are asked to undertake..

A foolproof solution is to treat everyone as though they are the recruiters. This means, not behaving in a way which you wouldn't want recruiters to see and not saying things you wouldn't want the recruitment officers to hear.

Leaving the venue

Leaving the venue, whether successful or not, is still a very crucial moment because you will be departing with other candidates, and undercover recruiters. If your behaviour becomes less desirable when you think it's all over, you could affect your chances of being offered a position either now, or in the future.

Final note

The fact is, these undercover recruiters are the reason why 90% of candidates fail at the group stage and it is, therefore, very important that no matter how confident you feel that another candidate is genuine, you must treat everyone with the same positive manner and never let your guard down.

Even if you don't encounter undercover recruiters, by treating everybody with the same positive attitude, you can never be judged negatively.

What Airlines Look For

Airlines are looking for candidates who use their initiative, remain calm under pressure, work well within a team, provide good customer care and can communicate competently with a variety of people.

During the day, recruitment officers will be looking for these desired qualities by assessing your involvement, behaviour and personality.

Activities

Generally, group assessments will span an entire day and involve several sessions. Successful progression through each stage will require participation in a number of tasks.

The following elements of the group interview process outline only what is common to some airlines. The formats airlines follow are incredibly diverse and are frequently changed, not all elements will be used by all airlines and the sequence in which they are carried out will vary.

Question & answer session

At some stage, usually early in the process, it is probable that the recruiters will give the group an opportunity to present any questions they have.

If you feel confident and have an appropriate question, this session is a fantastic opportunity to stand out and shine. If, on the other hand, your are feeling too overwhelmed, or simply don't have any questions, you should remain neutral and just listen at this stage.

If you do decide to pose a question, one is more than sufficient to get you noticed. You wouldn't want to show all your winning hands just yet.

You should avoid asking questions that are based on money and benefits as these will make you appear selfishly motivated. Instead, you should ask questions about the work and the airline. This will make you appear motivated and genuinely interested.

A list of suitable questions can be found of page 239.

Self-introduction

During a self-introduction, the recruiters will be assessing how well you cope, how well you communicate your message, and how comfortable you appear when addressing a group of people. They will also be looking for good delivery, and a certain amount of personal charisma.

The key to delivering a positive self presentation is to deliver your talk in an upbeat way that is enjoyable for others to listen to, thus, you should avoid learned-by-heart-speeches because they sound very boring and unprofessional. If you feel confident, you can inject some emotion and humour into your presentation. You could also use your hands and body language to emphasise points.

Try to talk naturally and positively, keeping it short and concise and mention things that will positively influence the recruiter's decision, such as why you are interviewing for the position, and what you have to offer.

You could say " Hi everyone. My name is Jane and it's really nice to meet you all. I'm 27 years old and live in the busy town of Any Town. I currently work as a freelance hair consultant, which is a job I really enjoy, but I have always wanted to be cabin crew, which is why I am here today. Besides working, I am a captain of my local football team, and am an avid horse rider."

By addressing everyone in this greeting, the candidate is showing a positive and confident attitude right from the start. She shares a few interesting facts about herself and her hobbies, which shows her personality outside of work, and then addresses her motives for making a career change.

Group discussion

Group discussions are very common during cabin crew assessments because they present an ideal opportunity for the recruiters to reveal which candidates are the leaders and followers, which candidates are arrogant or assertive, shy or confident, etc.

The topic of discussion may be hypothetical, or they may be based on current events. Either way, the topic and your opinion is largely irrelevant, it is your participation and attitude that count.

Remaining quiet at this crucial stage is really not an option, doing so will almost always guarantee your elimination.

Here are some sample hypothetical topics:

- 'The plane has gone down and there are 6 survivors: a priest, a nurse, a doctor, a child, a scientist and an expectant mother. The life raft will only carry three passengers, which three passengers would you save and why?'
- 'Discuss which famous people from world history you would invite to a dinner party and why?'

And here are some sample current event topics:

- 'What do you think about the ban on public smoking?'
- 'Do you think the USA and Great Britain should withdraw from Iraq?'

Group task

Group tasks take on many different forms and may involve role playing, problem solving scenarios, or even sing-alongs.

Airlines use these activities to assess how well you perform in a team environment, if you lead or follow, how well you think on your feet, how well you interact and consult with other members, if you make suggestions and how you react if your suggestion is not followed.

The tasks are designed to include an element of fun so you can expect them to be fairly simple in their design.

Here are some sample tasks:

- With the materials provided (i.e. paper, sticky tape and scissors), design and build a strong bridge that will support a full roll of sticky tape.
- With one candidate playing the role of an angry customer, show how you would diffuse the situation using a solution that the group has come up with.
- Using the pack of cards provided (the pack of cards may include various pictures such as paper cups, polo mints, ball of string etc…), discuss how you would use each of the items to entertain a group of passengers if you were stranded on a desert island. At the end of 20 minutes, you must present back to the recruitment team what you have chosen and why.
- In 15 minutes, write a song that will advertise the airline. Then perform the song to the grou

Tips for Success

The topic/task is irrelevant

The most important thing to bear in mind is that the topic or task is, to a certain extent, irrelevant. It is involvement, behaviour and personality which are really being assessed and how these qualities are applied in relation to the grou

The recruiters will be assessing how much you participate, how well you listen and what part you play in the grou

Be positive
Be positive about the exercises and tests you are asked to undertake. Those who show negative behaviour or are uncooperative will be rejected.

Volunteer
Volunteering is a great way to get the recruiters to notice you and also show you are keen to get involved and are not afraid to take the initiative.

Make suggestions
Making suggestions shows the recruiters that you are not afraid to express yourself and are keen to get involved. If, however, the group decides to go another way, don't take offence but get on board with your team and play your part in the activity.

Demand attention
Sometimes when you have a lot of different personalities in a group, some candidates may take over leaving other candidates, including you, unable to get a word in. Should you encounter this situation, you will need to employ some strategies to get involved.

The best way to get involved, without pushing your way in, is to simply raise your hand as you begin to speak. Raising your hand will demand the attention of the group and let them know that you have something to say.

In either case, say what you want to say and then hand the conversation over to another member of the team."What do you think Mark?"

Involve quieter members of the group
If there are members of the team who are reserved, it is a good idea to get them involved by asking what they think, or if they have any ideas. This shows empathy, a great quality for cabin crew.

Don't be afraid to disagree
If you disagree with an approach being taken by the group it is fine to speak up in a professional way. When done correctly, you will demonstrate that you are assertive, yet considerate of others opinions.

Consider the following example...

In response to the topic "What 5 items would you as a group take to on an exploration trip to the moon?" a candidate suggests a pen knife. In response to this, you reply "Yes - great idea! A knife is essential. How about we take a really multifunctional knife like a Swiss army knife?"

This is positive behaviour. It leads with the word 'yes'. The original idea is embraced and supported. A new idea is introduced in a non-threatening way, by seeking consensus and using the pronoun "we".

Selectors will be looking for positive behaviour such as this. They will also be looking at non-verbal signals, such as body language and tone of voice, to ascertain that the observed behaviour is genuine.

Summarise
There will undoubtedly come a point at which the ideas dry up and the discussion begins to go around in circles. The best thing to do in this situation is to summarise, "so where have we got so far". It is surprising how well summarising can get the discussion past the awkward moments of silence and back on track.

Speak strong and clear
This point is self explanatory; if you are talking too quiet, it may be perceived as shy (not a cabin crew quality).

Use people's names where possible
Using people's names is polite and shows a certain level of respect. Most importantly, when the recruiters give their names, be sure to remember them.

Bring humour to the group
If you feel comfortable and if it's appropriate humour, this will show the recruiters that you are comfortable being around new people and have a good sense of humour; it will also make the other candidates warm towards you, which has many benefits.

Keep track of time
If you are given a time limit for which to complete a particular task, this may be used as a test to see who remains aware of the time limit and who does not. Keep your eye on the time and when you have a

few minutes until the time is up, make sure the other candidates are alerted.

Common Mistakes to Avoid

Not getting involved or taking over
Those who cannot or will not get involved are not cabin crew material. For example: candidates who are too nervous, unable to put their point across, unwilling to commit, look bored, disinterested, aloof or bemused.

Equally, those who try to dominate or get over-involved are not suitable either. For example: Candidates who take control without seeking consensus, talk over or ignore the views of others, reject opinions because they do not agree with their own, or talk incessantly.

Good involvement is about achieving the right balance between expressing one's own opinions in a reasoned way, seeking consensus, and listening to/respecting the opinions of others.

Getting drawn into an argument
If something you say begins a debate with someone who disagrees with you, or vice versa, don't argue with the candidate but get other candidates involved by asking the group who also has an opinion on what you have said.

Disparaging others
Those who criticise, insult or make derogatory remarks about candidates, recruiters or past employers are certainly not desirable for any profession, let alone cabin crew, and doing so is a sure fire way of being eliminated.

Numeracy

While numeracy tests vary in difficulty, they are usually short and mostly designed to test your basic arithmetic skills: addition, subtraction, multiplication, and division.

If you haven't exercised your maths brain for some time, it may be a good idea to practice some basic mental arithmetic before the interview. Calculators may or may not be permitted.

Sample numeracy test questions

1. What is Twelve Thousand Nine Hundred and Seventy Six in figures?
A. 129,76.00   B. 12000976   C. 12,976.00

2. What is 6 multiplied by 8?
A. 48   B. 84   C. 56

3. Add 67 to 12
A. 80   B. 79   C. 76

4. You begin with a float of 66.94. A customer purchases a pack of peanuts at 0.66, a shot of spirits at 3.54 and a pack of chewing gum at 0.53. How much float should you have following this transaction?
A. 62.21   B. 71.76   C. 71.67

5. There are 357 seats on your aircraft. The seats are divided into 3 cabins. How many seats are in each cabin?
A. 117   B. 119   C. 109

Tips for success

- Run through your times tables
- Practice some basic calculations like subtraction and multiplication
- Practice estimating answers without the use of a calculator-
- Don't worry about complex math such as algebra. It is unlikely that you will be tested on this
- Read each question and answer carefully - sometimes multiple choice answers are deliberately similar so take time to check each option. Pay particular attention to things like the unit of measurement or the number of decimal places.

The Assessment Stage

Part 7

When completing any kind of aptitude test, it is important that you read the questions through fully and make sure you completely understand what is being asked before attempting to answer.

To be confident that you have answered as many questions as possible, it is always best to complete the questions you find easy on the first pass, returning to the trickier questions later.

To avoid handing in a form that is full of scribbles and mistakes, mark your answers out in pencil and carry out a final proof-read before you hand in your form.

Psychometric

Psychometric tests build a profile of characteristics, behavioural styles and personality, thus providing airlines with a clear assessment of a candidate's character and their ability to carry out a job.

Consequently, candidates try to imagine how the employer wants them to be and then answer the questions in such a way as to give a favourable impression.

My heartfelt advice is to answer the questions as honestly as possible because the test is only a supplementation to back up the recruiters own observations of you at the interview. If your actions or behaviour don't match up to your answers, it will become obvious that you have falsified your answers.

Sample psychometric test questions

For each question, you would give a mark out of five, One = Disagree strongly. Five = Agree strongly

- I enjoy meeting new people.
- I get bored doing repetitive tasks.
- I often lose my temper when I am frustrated.
- I always think before I act.
- I work well under pressure.
- I find it easy to relax.
- I get on well with most people.
- I am a teamplayer.
- I am very independent.
- I like to work alone.
- I become nervous in social situations.
- I find it difficult to communicate with other cultures.
- I thrive on challenges.

Language

If a second language is a requirement of the airline or if English isn't your native language, you may be required to complete a language assessment based on the following four key skills:

- Listening
- Reading
- Writing
- Speaking

Performance will be evaluated by how well the candidate understands (comprehension) and can be understood (comprehensibility).

Listening
In this section of the test, you will have the chance to show how well you understand the spoken language.

Questions you may come across are as follows:

- You will see a picture, and you will hear four short statements. When you hear the statements, look at the picture and choose the statement that best describes what you see in the picture.
- You will hear a question or statement, followed by three responses. You are to choose the best response to each question or statement.
- You will hear a short conversation between two people. You will then read a question about each conversation. The question will be followed by four answers. You are to choose the best answer to each question.

Reading
In this section of the test, you will have the chance to show how well you understand the written language.

Here are some examples...

The questions consist of incomplete sentences. Four words or phrases, marked (A), (B), (C) and (D), are given beneath each sentence. You are to choose one word or phrase that best completes the sentence.

Example:
Because the equipment is very delicate, it must be handled with
_____.

(A) Caring   (B) Careful   (C) Care   (D) Carefully

Each question in this section consists of a sentence that has four words or phrases underlined. The four underlined parts of the sentence are marked (A), (B), (C) and (D). You are to identify one underlined word or phrase that should be corrected or rewritten.

Example:
All <u>employees</u> are <u>repaired</u> to wear their <u>identification</u> badges while <u>at</u> work.

(A) employees   (B) repaired   (C) identification   (D) at

Writing & Speaking
In the written and spoken sections of the test, you will have the chance to show how well you speak and write the language.

You may be asked basic questions about your home town, family, work or study, leisure and future plans.

General Knowledge

General knowledge tests are not very common. If they are used, they are usually fairly straightforward.

Sample general knowledge test questions

- In relation to time, what does the abbreviation GMT stand for?
- How many continents are there?
- What is the name of the highest mountain in the world?
- Which is the largest continent?
- What is the capital of the USA?
- In which country would you find the river Nile?
- In which continent would you find Russia?

Reach

If the airline doesn't have a minimum height, they may have a reach test instead. The test demonstrates your ability to reach necessary places within the cabin and involves reaching up to touch a line on the wall. Your shoes will be removed for this test.

The reach requirement is usually 6'10" or 212cm. To determine your reach limit, simply measure out the distance from the floor and mark it out on your wall. If you can reach the mark in bare feet, you will surely pass any reach test.

Medical

You may be required to complete a short pre-employment medical questionnaire. This form is simply to confirm that you don't have a history of serious illness, or drug and alcohol abuse.

Complete the pre-employment questionnaire as accurately as possible. Don't lie or leave out important information as it will be evident when the full medical examination is carried out by the airline.

Affirming certain conditions isn't an automatic failure of your application, so if a condition has been treated or is being successfully controlled, clearly state this.

Aspire Airlines

Pre-employment medical questionnaire

Please ensure all sections of this form are completed. Failure to do so will cause delays.

Confidential

Declaration

I can verify that I am not aware of any medical condition that currently would prohibit my completion of the physical aspects of the training course or ongoing employment as a cabin crew member.

I hereby declare that the answers to the questions on this form are correct to the best of my knowledge and belief, and that I have not withheld any relevant information or made any misleading statement. I understand that incorrect answers may prejudice my employment with Aspire Airlines.

I am aware that further action may be required to investigate a medical condition and that additional information will be provided to me in relation to this at a later date, if applicable.

Date: 20/1/2009   Signature: /h   Printed name: JANE DOE

Present Address	**Permanent Address** *(if different)*
22 ANY STREET ANY TOWN	N/A
Post code AN2 6DG Country UNITED KINGDOM	Post code Country

Please give telephone number in the format: Country Code + City/Mobile Code + Phone Number

Telephone (Residence): 44 020 374693	Telephone (Residence):
Telephone (Mobile): 44 7509 283799	Telephone (Mobile):
Email: J.DOE@HOTMAIL.COM	

Position sought/ position held: CABIN CREW
Sex: FEMALE   Date of Birth: 11/09/1979
Height (without shoes): 154cm   Weight (without shoes) 49 kg
Colour of hair: BROWN   Colour of eyes: BLUE

Your Health Practitioner

Name: DR SHARON M ANDREWS
ANY HEALTH CENTRE

Please give telephone number in the format: Country Code + City Code + Phone Number

75 ANY ROAD   Telephone : 44 020 846738
ANY TOWN   Fax: 44 020 479055
Email: S.M.ANDREWS@ANYHEALTH.COM

Post code AN2 5HE   Country UNITED KINGDOM

Figure 12: Sample Pre-Employment Medical Examination Form - Page 1

Please continue your answers to the following questions on a separate sheet if necessary.

Have you ever been rejected or discharged from any form of employment for medical reasons? *If 'yes' state where, when and why.*

⟹ NO

Have you lost time from work in excess of one week on account of illness or injury? *If 'yes' state approx. dates, time lost and reasons.*

⟹ YES. I CAME DOWN WITH FLU DURING CHRISTMAS 2007 AND WAS AWAY FROM WORK FOR 9 DAYS

How much time have you had off work due to illness in the last 2 years? *State number of occasions and reasons.*

⟹ 9 DAYS. FLU DURING CHRISTMAS 2007

Have you ever received disability payments? (including National Health Benefits) *If 'yes' give details.*

⟹ NO

Have you ever received compensation for any illness or injury sustained at work? *If 'yes' give details.*

⟹ NO

Have you ever been a patient in a hospital, nursing home, clinic, mental hospital or institution? *If 'yes' where, when and why.*

⟹ NO

Are you suffering from any physical illness or disease at this time? *If 'yes' give details.*

⟹ NO

Are you taking or do you routinely take any drugs or medications? *If 'yes' give details (this includes contraceptive pill if applicable).*

⟹ YES. I HAVE THE DEPO PROVERA CONTRACEPTIVE PILL INJECTION EVERY 3 MONTHS SINCE 2005

Do you drink alcohol? *If 'yes' what is your average weekly intake in units?*

⟹ NO

Do you smoke? If 'yes' in what form and quantity.

⟹ NO

Do you, or have you ever had alcohol, drug or substance abuse? *If 'yes' please give details.*

⟹ NO

Do you or have you ever suffered with gynaecology/menstrual/abdominal/pelvic problems? *If 'yes' please give details.*

⟹ NO

Figure 13: Sample Pre-Employment Medical Examination Form - Page 2

Please continue your answers to the following questions on a separate sheet if necessary.

Are you suffering or have you suffered from any condition that the airline should be made aware of? *If 'yes' please give details.*

⟹ NO

Has your weight changed by more than 5kg (12lb) in the last 12 months? *If 'yes' give details.*

⟹ NO

Do you suffer or have you suffered from any back problems?

⟹ NO

As part of your contract of employment it will be necessary for you to maintain a yellow fever immunisation. *Please advise us if and when you have received this.*

⟹ YES RECEIVED IN 1994

Do you have hearing difficulties? *If 'yes' please give details.*

⟹ NO

Do you have normal eyesight with/without glasses/ contact lenses?

⟹ YES

Have you ever resided or otherwise associated with any person suffering from tuberculosis? *If 'yes' state where and when.*

⟹ NO

Have you any family history of high blood pressure, heart disease, hypertension, diabetes, or cancer? *If 'yes' please give details.*

⟹ YES, MY GRANDMOTHER AND MOTHER BOTH HAVE TYPE 2 DIABETES.

Have you ever experienced any symptoms of deafness or ear discomfort after air travel?

⟹ NO

Have you ever suffered from thrombosis or blood clots in the leg, or other blood disorders?

⟹ NO

Allergies

	Yes No	Severity of reactions if 'yes'
Drugs	NO	
Antibiotics	NO	
Bites	NO	
Stings	NO	
Nuts	NO	
Other (please specify) NON-BIO DETERGENT	YES	BUMPY RASH ON FACE

Figure 14: Sample Pre-Employment Medical Examination Form - Page 3

Please continue your answers to the following questions on a separate sheet if necessary.

Do you suffer from or have a history of:

	Yes No	If 'yes' give details
Nervous breakdown or mental illness?	No	
Frequent headaches or migraine?	No	
Head injury or concussion?	No	
Fits, convulsions or epilepsy?	No	
Tuberculosis?	No	
Pneumonia, bronchitis or other lung problems?	No	
Asthma?	No	
Hayfever or other allergy?	No	
Heart/vascular conditions?	No	
Chest pain?	No	
Undue shortness of breath?	No	
Swelling of ankles?	No	
High/low blood pressure?	No	
Fainting attacks/dizziness or unconsciousness?	No	
Rheumatic fever?	No	
Stomach pain or chronic indigestion?	No	
Peptic ulcer or abdominal pain?	No	
Bowel trouble?	No	
Kidney or bladder disease?	No	
Passing blood in urine or motions?	No	
Diabetes or endocrine disorder?	No	
Frequent colds/sinus trouble/nose or throat disorders?	No	
Earache or ear discharge?	No	
Skin disease (e.g. eczema, psoriasis etc)?	No	
Motion sickness?	No	
Muscle or joint pain?	No	
Surgical operations or injuries?	No	

Figure 15: Sample Pre-Employment Medical Examination Form - Page 4

The Final Interview Stage

Part 8

What to expect

Length of interview

There appears to be no set rule with regards to the length of time a final interview will last. You may be in and out within just 20 minutes, or the process may last for for one or two hours.

Either way, it will be nearly impossible to gauge your success based purely on the length of your interview because a short interview isn't necessarily a sign of failure. I personally know of several cases where a candidate has been successful after being interviewed for only 20 minutes.

Number of recruiters
Two recruitment officers are the general standard, however, things can and do change so you should be prepared for anything.

The process
The interview will generally begin with questions that are designed to ease you into the interview and make you feel relaxed. Questions about your current job – what you do, what your responsibilities are, etc, are common at this stage.

The recruiter will then seek to explore your motivation for applying to the airline. Questions such as 'What do you know about the airline, 'How do you feel about relocating' and 'Why do you want to become cabin crew' can be expected.

With the interview thoroughly under way, the recruiters will want to determine if you possess the skills required and are suitable for the position. Here you can expect more probing situational questions based on your work experience, such as 'When have you gone out of your way for a customer?', 'When have you been criticised about your work?', 'When have you worked as a team,' etc...

Tips for success

Remember, you are interviewing them too
Interviews are two-way exchanges. While recruiters are trying to determine if you are suitable for the job and the airline, you too need to determine if the airline is the right fit for you. Does the airline have the kind of values and environment you would be happy working in? Bearing this in mind may help you to relax.

Smile
A genuine and sincere looking smile will put others at ease around you. It will also give the impression that you are someone who is warm, welcoming, happy and confident.

Tip: If you can't fake it, just think about how lucky the recruiters are to be meeting you.

Stay focused

If you are thinking about how you look, what you are going to say next or have you failed, you will only make yourself nervous, and you may even misunderstand the question being asked.

You need to be completely focused on what the recruiters are saying in order to be able to remain composed and give the best possible answers.

Listen to the entire question before responding

This if for two reasons; first, you may assume that you know the answer before the recruiter finishes asking the question, but you may be surprised to find that the recruiter was going to ask a different question entirely. Second, if you interrupt the recruiter whilst they are talking, it shows disrespect. Be patient and you will have time to respond in due course.

Ask for clarification

If you are unsure, or feel you have misunderstood a question, it is better to request the recruiter to repeat, rephrase or summarise the question than to answer the question incorrectly.

Rather than jump straight in with your question, though, you should consider using a polite introductory phrase, such as:

- I beg your pardon but I don't quite follow/understand. I wonder if you could rephrase that in a different way?
- Do you think you could repeat the part about...once again please?
- Pardon me. Would you mind repeating that?
- Sorry, but I'm not sure I'm following you.
- Let's see if I understand/understood you correctly. ...
- Do you/Does this mean then that...
- Would it be correct to say that...
- So in other words...

Give short answers

If an answer is too long-winded, the recruiter will become complacent. Try to reveal as much information as you can with the least amount of words as possible.

Vary your tone to add interest

When the tone of your voice varies, it makes what you are saying more interesting. If your voice is monotone, it may be perceived as though you are not enthusiastic. It can also make the recruiters not want to listen.

Use emotion and humour

If you feel confident, and if it's appropriate, you can inject some emotion and humour into your answer. By doing this simple thing, you will sound and come across as genuine and will also keep the recruiters interested in what you are saying.

Be an active listener

Although you should never interrupt the recruiter, this doesn't mean listening in total silence. Instead, you should use active listening, which involves giving feedback via verbal cues. This feedback indicates to the recruiter that you are listening, and that you understand, thus the recruiter will feel encouraged to continue.

Maintain eye contact

Regular, strong eye contact will give the impression of someone who is honest and confident.

Where there is more than one recruitment officer, you should maintain eye contact with the person who asks you the question while occasionally engaging eye contact with the second recruiter .

Tip: If direct eye contact is too much, look at the bridge of the nose.

Use Mirroring

Mirroring is what happens when you have developed a rapport with another person and your body subconsciously, yet subtly, copies the movements and gestures of the other person.

If you are able to use mirroring techniques without being obvious, you will establish a better rapport with the recruiter.

Maintain positive body language

Your body language conveys all sorts of messages and the right body language will convey the message of a well-balanced confident individual, even if you are not.

Please refer to page 62 for further detailed advice.

Use silence
When you talk to the recruiter or answer his/her questions, use pauses to emphasize your point and to build up eager anticipation for what you are going to say next.

Structure
The recruiters have to be able to follow each stage of your answer in a logical sequence, so start at the beginning, and end at the end.

Mistakes to avoid

Verbal ticks
Anyways, you know how when you are, like, really nervous, and you ,ummm, find it hard to verbalise and stuff and you say silly things that, kind of, make you sound, like, kind of, unprofessional and maybe, like, inarticulate?

The useless and annoying verbal mannerisms used in the above example "you know," "like," "in other words," "kind of," "ummm," and "anyways." should be avoided at all costs. Besides making you sound unprofessional, they also distract attention from your message.

Unclear speech
You should make a conscious effort to slow the pace of your speech and enunciate clearly. Speaking too fast, or mumbling will make you harder to understand and definitely hurt your chances.

Getting sidetracked
When giving your answer, keep the information relevant and don't go off topic as there is a risk of losing track of your answer, which creates a negative impression about your communication skills.

Trying to lead or control
Don't try to lead or control the conversation, this is the recruitment officer's Job. You can, however, ask questions of your own when opportunities arise.

Interrupting the recruiter
Unless absolutely necessary, you should never interrupt the recruiter while they are speaking. Write down any questions or comments you have for later.

Shaking hands with sweaty palms

If this is something you have a problem with, try using talcum powder and keep a hanky close to hand.

Lying

If you lie, there is a good chance that your body language will give you away, leaving the recruiter not totally convinced by what you have said. Consequently, they may probe further with tricky follow-up questions, and if this happens, you could get caught out and end up looking very stupid. Clearly, if this happens, your chances of being offered the job will be ruined.

Panicking

If your mind goes blank, don't panic and say the first thing that comes into your head. Breathe deeply and play for time by saying something like 'that's an interesting question', this will give you time to collect your thoughts,

Being negative

There is no room for negativity when it comes to interviews of any kind. Be especially careful about being negative about other jobs, airlines, people, previous employers and your current job.

Breaking silence unnecessarily

Some recruiters use silence as a tool for eliciting further response from a candidate. Once you say what you wanted to say, they will leave you in limbo for a few, very long seconds. You must resist the urge to say something just to break that silence.

Taking negative questions personally

Sometimes, recruiters will ask a series of negative questions such as 'How would you react if I told you that your presentation this afternoon was lousy?' or 'How would you respond if I told you that your skills/experience are below the requirements of this position?' Don't take these types of questions personally as the recruiters are asking them to get a reaction from you. Your reaction should be a positive one that reinforces the reasons why the airline should hire you.

Smoking

Even if it is allowed, try not to smoke at any time during the interview process. Many airlines will not consider applicants who smoke due to the non-smoking environments you will be working in. Also, the smell of smoke will linger on your clothing, which can be unpleasant.

Questions & Answers

Part 9

Cabin crew interview questions are fairly unique because the questioning tends to focus almost exclusively on personal qualities and experiences. As a result, there are no definite right or wrong answers, just more appropriate answers and better forms of expression.

It is important to have examples ready, to back up any statements made, for example, "I enjoy providing customer care" may be investigated with the question "When have you provided good customer care?" or perhaps a statement like "I appreciate there are times when a crew member has to remain calm under pressure" would be followed with the question "When have you experienced a pressured situation?"

Within the following pages, I have listed various interview questions, followed by examples of effective ways to answering each of them in a detailed, yet concise manner.

Please remember...
The answers provided on the following pages are designed to be used as a guide to assist you in formulating your own answers and should not be copied in their entirety.

Contents
At a Glance...

Competency Questions...

Customer Focus

Communication Competence

Initiative

Decision Making & Problem Solving

Teamwork & Working Relationships

Managing Adversity

Stress Tolerance

Competency questions are based on personal experiences, which demonstrate a particular set of skills that the airline has pre-determined are necessary for the job.

By knowing how you have behaved and applied certain skills in the past, they can determine that you possess the required skills and predict how you will behave in the future.

The SARR Formula

The SARR formula is a technique that you can use to formulate a more detailed answer. The more complete your answer is, the less recruiters will need to probe further with follow-up questions.

SARR stands for:

Situation   Begin by briefly describing the challenge, problem, achievement or task

Action   Go on to describe what actions you took to solve the problem, face the challenge or complete the task?

Result   Describe the outcome and how your actions affected the outcome or people involved

Reflection   Finally, you may want to explain how your actions affected the other person and/or outcome, and what you learned from the experience.

Here is an example of an answer which follows this formula:

Situation
"I recently experienced a situation with a client who was having relationship problems and who became very emotional. I could sense that she was feeling very depressed, and I tried to think of what I could do to hel"

Action
"Although I felt compassion for her situation, I knew that it was important to not get too involved. I gave her chance to talk while I listened, and I tried to show empathy while remaining neutral and professional in my response."

Result

"Just being able to talk things through with someone who listened seemed to make her feel better. As she gained a deeper insight into her situation, she began seeing things more positively. Consequently, she was able to calmly discuss her feelings with her partner and work through their problems. She later thanked me for listening. It made me feel good that I could make such a big difference. She's now a regular client of mine and is still happily married."

Reflection

"From this experience, I learned that just listening can be providing good customer care and ultimately change someone's future to a more positive one."

Preparing examples

Airlines are looking for candidates who use their initiative, remain calm under pressure, work well within a team, provide good customer care and can communicate competently with a variety of people. Thus, they will be looking for examples, which demonstrate your use of each of those skills.

With this in mind, you should try to prepare at least one example for each key area, focusing not only on positive examples but also on negative experiences too.

The examples you select should be true and not exaggerated, and they should be detailed, yet brief.

In the case of negative experiences, you need to be very selective about your choices. Never provide a negative example that involves a core skill, nor one which had an undesirable impact on the company, colleagues or customers. You will also want to turn the negative experience into a positive one by demonstrating how it became a valuable learning experience.

Follow-up questions

Recruiters may probe deeper into your answers with follow-up questions. Prepare to be asked:

- What did you learn from the experience?
- What specifically did you say?
- How did you feel?
- Would you do anything differently?
- How did they react?
- What other options did you consider?
- Why did you decide to take the action that you did?
- You mentioned _____. Tell me more about that.
- How did you retain your composure?
- Can you give me an example of that?
- Can you be more specific about _____?

Lack of relative experience

If you don't have relative experience in a particular area, you need to be honest and say so. Remind the recruiter of the skills you do have and describe how you would handle the situation.

You could say, "I can't remember ever being in that situation, however, I did face something slightly similar that I could tell you about?"

Customer
Focus...

1 When have you provided good customer service?

Evaluation

Being able to provide excellent customer service is vital to the role of cabin crew, so you should have plenty of real life examples ready to share. This is your chance to shine, so don't be modest.

Sample Response

Introduction:

I always take great pride in providing the very best service I possibly can, however, I do recall a particular experience when I was particularly happy with the service I provided.

Situation:

I was in the staff room during my lunch break, and I could hear a lot of noise coming from inside the salon. I went to investigate and I was confronted by two young, and very bored, children. I could sense that the situation was causing an inconvenience for not only their mother, who was having a conditioning treatment, but also the stylist.

Action:

I decided to take the initiative and see what I could do to occupy the children. I sat them down and asked if they would like to have their hair plaited like a princess. Their eyes lit up and they jumped at the chance. After finishing their hair, we made shiny bead bracelets from some hair beads.

Result:

We had lots of fun and they really enjoyed themselves. Consequently, the client and the stylist had a stress free time.

Reflection:

I felt really pleased that with just a little extra effort, I had made such a difference.

2 When could your customer service have been better?

Evaluation

Providing excellent customer service is vital to the role of cabin crew, thus you should never volunteer negative customer service examples.

Consequently, you should explain how you maintain your standards, and proceed with an example of a time when you have demonstrated this capability.

Sample Response

I take great pride in providing the best service I possibly can, and I never let my standards sli Even during times of high pressure, I make an effort to remain courteous and helpful. I can honestly say that I have never received any negative feedback.

Take the example of when my client's perm fell out because she had gone against my written instructions. First she denied receiving the instructions, and then she began slandering my service and the salon. Although everything worked out well in the end, it could have been so easy to let standards slip in such a situation, but I remained calm and assertive, and never let my emotions cloud my judgement.

3 When have you gone out of your way for a customer?

Evaluation

In the airline business, the customer's satisfaction is the key to success. Those candidates who demonstrate that they always put in extra effort to provide a better and more complete service will surely have an advantage.

Sample Response

Situation:
I remember a client was asking for a particular product that she had seen advertised, but had been unable to locate in any shops.

Action:
I knew I could get this product from the wholesalers, but it was not available for purchase by the general public, so I offered to assist by purchasing the product on her behalf.

Result:
She was very grateful for my efforts, which gave me a sense of self satisfaction.

4 When have you solved a customer problem?

Evaluation

The recruiter wants to get an idea of how you apply your initiative and problem-solving skills to customer related issues.

A good answer here will demonstrate that you always put in extra effort to provide good customer service and are not intimidated by difficult situations.

Sample Response

Introduction:
In my profession, I solve customer problems all the time. I do, however, remember one problem in particular.

Situation:
I had a client who had worn sewn in hair extensions for three years. The extensions had been placed so tightly that they had caused damage to the clients natural hair and spots of baldness.

Action:
After applying a deep conditioning treatment, I carefully applied some fresh extensions to conceal the bald patches and sent her home with a concentrated protein spray.

Result:
Within two weeks the client's hair began to feel healthy again, and she had tons of new growth. Needless to say, she is very happy.

5 When have you bent the rules for a customer?

Evaluation

There are situations, such as in the example below, where it is permissible to bend the rules. However, the airline may view rule bending negatively, no matter how trivial or well intended. Consequently, you may wish to play it safe by declaring: "I have always abided by company policies and have never bent the rules."

If you do decide to provide an answer, you should show that you are able to keep balance between company policy and the interest of customers;

Sample Response

Introduction:
Working freelance, the idea is to provide the service within the client's premises.

Situation:
I encountered a problem when one of my clients was unable to have the service carried out in her home because it was being renovated.

Action/Result:
In an attempt to retain the client, I spoke a contact I had within a local salon and managed to make an arrangement to carry out the service within the salon for a small fee. This worked out really well because it was convenient for both myself and the client to travel to.

When have you experienced an upset customer?

Evaluation

The recruiter is trying to grasp your ability to cope with stressful situations. A good answer will suggest that you can think on your feet, and display a positive and patient attitude when challenging situations arise.

Sample Response

Situation:

I recently experienced a situation with a client who was having relationship problems and who became very emotional. I could sense that she was feeling very depressed, and I tried to think of what I could do to hel

Action:

Although I felt compassion for her situation, I knew that it was important to not get too involved. I gave her chance to talk while I listened, and I tried to show empathy while remaining neutral and professional in my response.

Result:

Just being able to talk things through with someone who listened seemed to make her feel better. As she gained a deeper insight into her situation, she began seeing things more positively. Consequently, she was able to calmly discuss her feelings with her partner and work through their problems. She later thanked me for listening.

Reflection:

It made me feel good that I could make such a big difference. She's now a regular client of mine and is still happily married.

From this experience, I learned that just listening can be providing good customer care and ultimately change someone's future to a more positive one.

7 When have you been confronted by an irate customer?

Evaluation

This type of customer is perhaps the most difficult to deal with and the recruiter wants to assess whether or not you can deal with confrontational issues in a calm and rational manner.

You will be assessed on how well you coped under the pressure and how you dealt with the customer. A good response will show that you never lost your temper and remained courteous throughout the experience.

If you haven't experienced such a situation, you migh say "Thankfully, this is a situation I haven't experienced, however, I could imagine my response if you would like?" You could then proceed to explain how you would appraoch the situation.

Sample Response

Situation:
Shortly after I began freelancing, I encountered a problem when an associate of mine tried to pressure me into a free hair service based on friendshi

Action:
I proceeded to offer her, what I considered to be, a reasonable discount, but she was not satisfied with my offer, and proceeded to pressure me with emotional blackmail. I remained cordial, but became more assertive as I continued to refuse her demands.

Result:

Rather than accept the reasons for my decision, she became increasingly enraged, and even began to slander my service and friendshi

Shocked at her over-reaction, and concerned about what might develop, I felt I had no option but to withdraw from the situation.

Reflection:

This experience was very challenging, and certainly tested my patience, but I remained calm and, although this particular relationship never recovered, it was a learning experience that, thankfully, hasn't since been repeated.

8 When have you experienced a difficult customer?

Evaluation

The ability to remain well mannered and well tempered while dealing with a difficult customer is an absolute necessity for cabin crew.

A good response will show that you remained calm and courteous throughout the experience, and were able to create a satisfactory outcome.

Sample Response

Introduction:

If by difficult, you mean challenging then yes, I do remember one challenging customer in particular.

Situation:

I remember when a client came into the salon requesting a full colour treatment. She had attempted a home bleaching treatment, which had gone terribly wrong, and was desperate to have the colour fixed.

Action:

Unfortunately, when checking the client's hair, I determined that it was extremely dry and over-processed. Concerned that another treatment would damage the clients hair beyond repair, I decided to carry out a strand test. The strand test confirmed my suspicions as the hair practically fell apart in my hands. Based on the evidence, I advised the customer that I was unprepared to carry out the treatment

Result:

Understandably, the client was very upset, but instead of accepting my decision, she began begging for me to carry out the treatment. She even insisted that she would sign a disclaimer.

Sympathetic of her situation, I listened to what she had to say, but remained assertive in my decision as I explained that my decision was for her benefit.

Unfortunately, the client was too overcome with her emotions and eventually stormed out of the salon.

Reflection:

This was a very difficult position to be put in, but I remained calm and courteous, and made the decision for the interests of the client.

9 When have you handled a customer complaint?

Evaluation

The recruiter wants to know that you are able to retain your composure and use your problem solving skills when dealing with a dissatisfied customer.

A good response will show that you never took the complaint personally, remained calm and courteous, and were able to create a satisfactory outcome for the customer.

Sample Response

Situation:
I remember when I was working as a receptionist, and a client rang to complain about a perm that she had had done.

Action:
I could sense that the customer was very unhappy, so I gave her my undivided attention while she proceeded to explain what the problem was. Once she had calmed down, I calmly apologised for the situation and immediately offered her an appointment to have the perm fixed, she agreed.

Result:
The customer returned to the salon later that day, and had some slight re-perming done. In under an hour, she left the salon happy with the result, and thanked me for my prompt and supportive response.

10 When have you had to say 'No' to a customer?

Evaluation

As cabin crew, there will be occasions when it is necessary to say no to a passenger, and the recruiter wants to know that you aren't intimidated by such situations and have the strength of character to deal with the situation authoritatively, yet diplomatically.

You will be assessed on how you how you approached the customer and went about dealing the situation.

A good response will demonstrate your ability to use tact, and will show that you remained courteous throughout the experience.

Sample Response

Situation:

I had a client booked in for highlights, but after examining her hair I noticed she had a very dry scal As the safety of my clients is important to me, I was not prepared to carry out the treatment until her scalp had healed. Understandably, the client was very upset, and she tried to persuade me to change my mind.

Action:

Sympathetic of her situation, I listened to what she had to say, but remained assertive in my decision as I explained that my actions were for her protection. I then apologised for the inconvenience, and provided her with a deep moisturising solution.

Result:

After using the solution consecutively, I was able to return to carry out the treatment just four days later.

The client later thanked me for my honesty and concern.

11 | Describe a situation when the customer was wrong?

Evaluation

Although the popular saying suggests otherwise, the customer isn't always right and the recruiter wants to know that you aren't Intimidated by such situations and are able to handle such customers diplomatically, yet authoritatively.

You will be assessed on how you how you approached the customer and went about dealing the situation. A good response will demonstrate your ability to use tact, and will show that you remained courteous throughout the experience.

Sample Response

Situation:
I remember one customer in particular who I had carried out a perming treatment for. After completing the treatment, I provided written instructions for how to care for her new perm which specifically instructed against washing the hair for at least 48 hours.

Unfortunately, the very next day, the client washed her hair and the perm significantly dropped on one side. The client was understandably very upset, but refused to accept that the perm had fallen out as a consequence of her actions. She then started to slander my work and the salon.

Action:
When asked if she had followed the instructions, she denied being provided with any. I assured her that instructions were provided, and suggested she check her belongings.

Result:
Later that afternoon, the client returned to the salon holding onto the instruction sheet with a very embarrassed look on her face. She apologised profusely for her behaviour.

12 When have you had to resolve a conflict between what the customer wanted and what you could realistically deliver?

Evaluation

Here, the recruiter wants to determine that you have the strength of character to voice your concerns and also the communication skills necessary to be diplomatic, yet authoritative, in voicing those concerns.

You will be assessed on how you how you approached the customer and how you dealt with the situation.

Sample Response

Situation:

I remember a client who came in for a colour treatment and restyle. She had used a virtual hairstyle software to create her ideal look, and was beaming with excitement as she showed me the picture and declared, "This is what I want".

The style was notably very pretty, and it was clear that it was ideally suited to the client. Unfortunately, though, the client's hair had been through several colour treatments, and the platinum blonde shade that she wanted just wasn't going to be possible at that time.

Action:

Knowing how excited the client was, I felt a little dejected as I proceeded to break this news to her.

In the hope of relieving some of her obvious disappointment, I suggested a strand test to see if it would be possible to life some of the colour. If the strand test were a success, we could perform a gradual transformation through the use of highlights.

Result:

Thankfully, the strand test was a success, and the client, while disappointed, was happy to go ahead with the gradual transformation. The result was striking, and the client was happy with the result.

Every few months following, we put in more highlights and within nine months, the transformation was complete, and I had a very satisfied customer.

Communication
Competence...

13 When have you shown good communicative ability?

Evaluation

The ability to communicate with a wide range of people from different backgrounds is vital to the role of cabin crew, so you should have plenty of examples that demonstrate this ability.

Sample Response

Situation:

I remember when one of our trainees was having problems understanding certain aspects of her course material, and I could see she was becoming increasingly frustrated and self critical.

Action:

Having witnessed her in action, I knew that she was a very bright and talented individual with no obvious lack of skill. So I determined that her frustrations were probably the result of the pressure she was feeling about her approaching exam.

Concerned at the effect this pressure was having on her, and having experienced the same pressures myself, I could relate to her position and knew that what she probably needed was a break from the environment.

We went to lunch where I offered my support and encouragement. When she was feeling more relaxed, we returned to the salon where I reinforced her understanding by demonstrating some of the techniques she had struggled with.

Result:

My breakdown of the processes, along with the visual demonstration I provided, seemed to make the material much more understandable. In the days that followed, she seemed to have a new lease of life and was much more positive. Subsequently, she passed her exams with top grades.

14

When have you had to vary your communication style according to the person you were addressing?

Evaluation

As cabin crew, you will interact with a variety of people from a broad range of cultures and backgrounds on a daily basis. The ability to relate to others and adapt your communication style is, therefore, very important and so you should have plenty of examples readily available that demonstrate this ability.

Sample Response

Situation:

During a trip to Africa, I became acquainted with a French lady. She understood my French, the little amount I knew, but she didn't really understand English. Unfortunately, the amount of French I knew wasn't enough to get me through a whole conversation, so I had to improvise.

Action:

To ensure she could understand, I used French wherever possible, and made more use of facial expressions and hand gestures.

Result:

At first, it was a little tricky trying to find imaginative ways to communicate, but over time, I became much more proficient, and I came away with a new friend.

Reflection:

Now when I encounter this type of communication barrier, I am much more confident in my ability to cope.

15 When have your communication skills made a difference to a situation or outcome?

Evaluation

The ability to communicate well is vital to the role of cabin crew, so you should have plenty of examples that demonstrate this ability.

Sample Response

Situation:
I remember a trainee apprentice who never asked questions, and refused all offers of hel I guess she though it would make her look incompetent.

Unfortunately, instead of trying to understand her reasons, everyone drew the conclusion that she was a know-it-all, and vowed not to offer help in the future.

Action:
Concerned that her progress would suffer, I decided to spend some time with her so that I could offer encouragement and support. I explained that it was ok to ask questions, and mistakes were expected.

Result:
Very quickly after that, we saw a change in her behaviour. She began asking questions, she was more open to suggestions, and her skills improved immensely.

Reflection:
From this experience, I learn't that things are not always what they appear, thus it is good to question before making rash judgements.

16 When have you had to explain something complex to the customer or colleague?

Evaluation

As cabin crew, you may be required to break down and convey complex information to customers. For example, if a passenger is afraid of flying, you may need to explain the technicalities of the flight, or if a passenger is hasn't grasped the use of emergency equipment and emergency procedures, you may need to break the information down further.

Your answer here will show that you are able to express knowledge in a clear and simple manner.

Sample Response

Situation:
I remember a client who wanted to have a colour treatment done, but was concerned about the potential damage to her natural hair.

Action:
Not satisfied with a simple non-technical version, I had to provide a detailed technical breakdown of the process. This involved describing the molecular structure of the hair, the effect colour particles have, and how they bond to the structure.

Result:
Although I had to occasionally refer to training manuals to emphasise or clarify my point, overall the client was satisfied with my effort, and, as a direct result, she went ahead with the treatment and was very pleased with the outcome.

17 When have your listening skills helped resolve a situation?

Evaluation

Active listening not only allows you to make sense of and understand what another person is saying, it also allows you to build rapport and resolve problems with co-workers, bosses, and customers. Thus, the ability to use your listening skills actively and effectively is a vital skill for the role of cabin crew.

The recruiter will be looking to understand how you use your listening skills in relation to problem solving.

You should have plenty of examples ready to demonstrate your listening ability.

Sample Response

Situation:

I recently experienced a situation with a client who was having relationship problems and who became very emotional. I could sense that she was feeling very depressed, and I tried to think of what I could do to hel

Action:

Although I felt compassion for her situation, I knew that it was important to not get too involved. I gave her chance to talk while I listened, and I tried to show empathy while remaining neutral and professional in my response.

Result:

Just being able to talk things through with someone who listened seemed to make her feel better. As she gained a deeper insight into her situation, she began seeing things more positively. Consequently, she was able to calmly discuss her feelings with her partner and work through their problems. She later thanked me for listening.

Reflection:

It made me feel good that I could make such a big difference. She's now a regular client of mine and is still happily married.

From this experience, I learned that just listening can be providing good customer care and ultimately change someone's future to a more positive one.

18 What was the toughest communication problem you have faced?

Evaluation

We all experience difficulties in communication, to say otherwise wouldn't sound honest or credible.

There are many reasons why communication may become difficult. It may be that one or both parties lack the ability to listen actively, conflict may be causing tension, there may be a language or hearing barrier, or it could be simply a case of an inability to articulate correctly.

Whatever the cause, the recruiter will be assessing how you approach such difficulties and how you use your initiative to come to a positive resolution.

A good answer here will show that you remained patient and used your initiative.

Sample Response

Situation:
Generally, I am a very efficient communicator, but I do recall when I experienced difficulty communicating with an OAP client.

Action:
The client was very hard of hearing, and I tried everything to communicate with her. I spoke slower, louder, used hand gestures and facial expressions, I even tried to write the information down, but without her glasses, she was unable see my writing clearly.

Result:
Fortunately, I managed to locate a magnifying glass, which enabled the client to read my instructions, and everything worked out well in the end.

19 When have you failed to communicate effectively?

Evaluation

We all experience challenges in communication, but a complete failure to communicate effectively will show a lack of initiative and creativity in problem solving.

Whatever the reason for a communication challenge, there is always a way to communicate if you are willing to put in some additional effort and your answer should reflect this.

If a customer is hard of hearing, you can use the written word; A language barrier would require the use of body language and facial expressions. A conflict could simply require the use of active listening and assertive speech.

Sample Response

While I have certainly encountered communication challenges, I can honestly say that I have never yet failed in my ability to communicate.

Sometimes it requires the use of all your initiative and creativity, but there is always a way around communication barriers.

For instance, with a language or hearing barrier, using the written word, along with emphasised body language and facial expressions often help in communicating your message and emphasising certain points.

Initiative...

20 | What have you done that shows initiative?

Evaluation

The recruiter is interested in your level of enthusiasm, energy and dedication.

Your answer here should show that you take the initiative when it comes to additional work and demonstrate a natural desire for doing extra tasks willingly.

Sample Response

Introduction:
At Any Hair Salon, I sometimes performed various tasks that were not, strictly speaking, a part of my job.

Situation:
For example, when I began working at the salon, the inventory system was outdated, and the storage room was very messy and disorganised.

Action:
I came in on my day off, cleaned up the mess, organised the store cupboards, and catalogued it all on the new inventory forms.

Result:
Thereafter when orders arrived, it was easy to organise and, therefore, retrieve.

Reflection:
If I'm able to do the task, instead of waiting for the job to be done, I simply do it.

21 Tell me about a time that you undertook a course of study, on your own initiative, in order to improve your work performance

Evaluation

The recruiter is interested in your level of enthusiasm, energy and dedication. They want to determine that you recognize areas that need development.

Your answer here should show that you are committed to self-development and take the initiative when it comes to improving yourself and your efficiency.

Sample Response

Situation:

While at Any Hair Salon, we were experiencing a spectacular rise in demand for high fashion cuts. I had some creative cutting experience, but nothing that extended to the kind of advanced skill that was required for true high fashion cuts.

Action:

After some consideration, I decided that increasing my creative cutting skills would not only give the salon a competitive advantage, but it would also be a fantastic opportunity for me to move my skills to the next level.

I looked around, and was lucky to find a local community college offering a short creative cutting course. I took the initiative, and, under my own funding, immediately enrolled.

Result:

My new skills proved to be an instant success. Existing clients began recommending me to their friends, which resulted in a massive rise in clientele. Needless to say, my manager was very happy.

22 | Describe an improvement that you personally initiated

Evaluation

The recruiter wants to know that you seek better and more effective ways of carrying out your work and can suggest improvements that will achieve more efficiency.

Your answer here should show that you take the initiative when it comes to improving working methods and standards.

Sample Response

Situation:

While traveling in India, I was taught the art of Indian head massage.

Action:

When I returned to work, I began using my new skill on clients while carrying out the shampoo.

Result:

My massages were becoming such a success, that my manager approached me to request that I train my colleagues. Naturally, I was honoured to oblige.

23 Describe a new idea or suggestion that you made to your supervisor

Evaluation

The recruiter wants to know that you seek better and more effective ways of carrying out your work and can suggest improvements that will achieve more efficiency.

Your answer here should show that you take the initiative when it comes to improving working methods and standards.

Sample Response

Situation:
When I was working at Any Hair Salon, I had noticed that a lot of our clients wore nail extensions.

Action:
Convinced that the service would be an improvement to our already successful salon, I carried out extensive independent research, and then presented the idea to my manager.

Result:
After carrying out her own research, she liked the idea so much that she decided to go ahead with the new service. Within a couple of months, the service was up and running, and we experienced a dramatic increase in new clientele and revenue. I even got a small bonus in my pay packet for my involvement.

Decision Making
& Problem Solving...

24 | Tell me about the biggest mistake you ever made

Evaluation

We all make mistakes, and to say otherwise will not sound honest or credible.

The recruiter will be assessing whether you have the character to admit and take responsibility for your mistakes, whether your mistake had a negative impact on customers or the company, and whether you learnt from this mistake?

In answering this question, you need to first ensure that the mistake was a minor one, which had no negative or lasting impact on the company or a customer. Try to accentuate the positives and keep your answer specific. Itemize what you did and how you did it. Finally, you need to make it clear that you learnt from the mistake and will be certain not to repeat it.

Sample Response

Situation:
The biggest mistake was providing my service to a friend on credit.

Action/Result:
Not only was it extremely difficult to retrieve the money, but once the message got around everybody else began expecting the same treatment.

Reflection:
Unfortunately, it really was my fault. I learned from the experience, and I have never repeated the mistake.

25 What was the most difficult decision you have made?

Evaluation

The recruiter will be assessing your ability to judge the situation, and think logically and wisely to arrive at a decision. They will want to see that you have a balanced thinking process, and are not too hasty in coming to a decision.

When answering this question, give a concrete example of a difficult decision that you faced, and then discuss how you arrived at your decision. Keep your answers positive and be specific.

Sample Response

Situation:
The decision to leave the comfort and security of my full time job to become freelance was definitely the hardest I have had to make.

Making the right decision required a lot of forethought and looking at best and worst case scenarios extensively before making my decision.

Action:
I carried out independent research and already had a few clients to start off with but still found the decision difficult because I knew that there are no guarantees that people will use the service.

Result:
Thankfully, I went ahead and the outcome was a positive one.

26 | What was the biggest challenge you have faced?

Evaluation

In answering this question, you need to provide a concrete example of a challenge you faced, and then Itemize the steps you took to overcome that challenge.

Your answer should display a patient and positive attitude when challenging situations occur.

Sample Response

Situation:
To be honest, giving up smoking was the biggest challenge. I never thought I could do it, and I had had dozens of attempts that ended in failure.

Action:
Determined not to give in to my withdrawals, I decided I needed an incentive that would pull me through the tough times. Being sponsored for a worthy cause was the perfect solution.

Result:
With a good cause in mind, the following three months were easier than on previous occasions. Not only have I come out the other end a non-smoker, I also managed to raise £2464.00 for Childline.

Reflection:
Since I gave up smoking, I have gained so much personal insight, and I deal with potentially stressful situations at work so much more effectively now, I feel more energetic, more mentally alert and far calmer now than I ever did before.

27 | When have you made a bad decision?

Evaluation

We all make decisions that we regret, and to say otherwise will not sound honest or credible.

The recruiter will be assessing whether you have the character to admit and take responsibility for your mistake, whether your decision had a negative impact on customers or the company, and whether you learnt from this mistake?

In answering this question, you need to first ensure that the mistake was a minor one, which had no negative or lasting impact on the company or a customer. Try to accentuate the positives and keep your answer specific. Itemize what you did and how you did it. Finally, you need to make it clear that you leant from the mistake and will be certain not to repeat it.

Sample Response

Situation:

Early in my freelance career, I was approached by a salesman who was promoting a protein conditioning system. He described the system as "The newest technology to emerge from years of research. Guaranteed to help heal, strengthen, and protect".

Although I was excited by the concept, I did have my concerns that the system sounded too good to be true. However, the salesman had all the official paperwork to back up his claims, and the literature was thorough and well presented. All these things, combined with the company's full money-back guarantee, made it appear to be a win-win situation, and a risk worth taking. So I invested.

Following my investment, I decided to test the system out on training heads before taking the system public. Unfortunately, several months of using the system passed with no obvious benefits. At this stage, it was becoming increasingly apparent that the system had been a complete waste of money.

Action:

Disappointed with the product, I decided to pursue the full money back guarantee.

To my surprise, their sales number was unrecognised, and my letters were returned unopened. Even their website had mysteriously vanished.

At this stage, the reality of the situation started to loom as it was becoming obvious that I had been part of an elaborate scam.

With no other avenues to explore, I decided to contact the Citizens Advice Bureau, who advised me to report the company to Trading Standards.

Unfortunately, while the Trading Standards had received several complaints about this company, there was little they could do to retrieve my funds.

Result:

Unfortunately, I never recovered my costs and had to put the mistake down to a learning experience.

Reflection:

Unfortunately, it really was my fault. I should have trusted my gut instinct and carried out thorough research before making my decision. It is a mistake I shall never repeat.

28 Tell me about a problem you encountered and the steps you took to overcome it

Evaluation

The recruiter will be assessing how well you cope with diverse situations, and how you use your judgment to solve problems.

In answering this question, you need to provide a concrete example of a problem you faced, and then Itemize the steps you took to solve the problem. Your answer should demonstrate a patient and positive attitude towards problem solving.

Sample Response

Situation:
Early in my freelancing career, I experienced several clients who turned up late to their appointments. Some even forgot about their appointments altogether. Rather than just simply being an inconvenience, it was wasting my time, and that meant I was also losing money.

Action:
I considered my options, and decided that the best solution would be to send out reminder cards a few days prior to client appointments, and for the repeat offenders, I would enforce a late cancellation fee.

Result:
With just a little extra time and effort, I drastically cut the number of late arrivers, and I have never since had a no-show.

Reflection:
There are always solutions to problems if you are willing to invest a little time and effort.

29 | Tell me about a problem that didn't work out

Evaluation

No matter how hard we try, there are some instances where a problem just doesn't work out. To say otherwise will not sound honest or credible.

In answering this question, you need to first ensure that the problem was a minor one, which had no negative or lasting impact on the company or a customer. Try to accentuate the positives and keep your answer specific. Itemize the steps you took to deal with the problem. Finally, you need to make it clear that you learnt from the experience.

Sample Response

Situation:
Shortly after I began freelancing, my bank returned a client's cheque to me through lack of funds.

Action:
I was sure it was a mistake caused through an oversight on the part of my client, so I made a number of calls, I left several messages, and finally, with no response, I visited her home. Several weeks passed, and it was becoming clear that I was chasing a lost cause. At this point, I had to decide whether to write off the debt and blacklist the client, or visit the Citizens' Advice for advice on retrieving the funds.

Result:
After careful consideration of all the factors involved, I decided to write the debt off as a learning experience.

Reflection:
In hindsight, I realise it was a silly mistake that could easily have been avoided. I have never repeated this error since as I now wait for the funds to clear before carrying out a service.

Teamwork
& Working
Relationships...

30 When have you worked successfully within a team?

Evaluation

The ability to work well within a team is absolutely essential to working as cabin crew. You should, therefore, have plenty of examples that demonstrate this ability.

Sample Response

Situation:

There was a particular time that stands out for me because it was such an unusual occurrence.

It was a usual quiet Tuesday afternoon, and only myself, another senior stylist, a trainee, and the salon manager were on duty. To our surprise, it was as if someone began offering out free chocolate, as clients started to filter through the doors.

Action:

Despite the overwhelming rush, we showed great teamwork as we pulled together and shared our duties. The trainee washed hair, and tended to clients and the reception area. Even our manager showed great team spirit as she got involved with colouring and cutting services.

Result:

As a result of our teamwork, and some free relaxing conditioning treatments, we managed to deliver an outstanding service, and every client went away completely satisfied with their hair and the service.

31 | Tell us about a challenge you have faced with a colleague

Evaluation

Airlines have a constant rotation of crew onboard each aircraft, and, especially within larger airlines, you may not work with the same crew-members twice. Due to this, it is guaranteed that you will encounter challenging situations with colleagues.

The recruiters want to know that you aren't intimidated by such colleagues or situations, and are prepared to use your initiative to diffuse or mediate as necessary to keep working relationships healthy.

Your answer should demonstrate your willingness to co-operate with others to resolve differences, improve relations, and manage conflicts. It should also display your ability to remain patient and positive in the face of adversity.

Sample Response

Situation:

I do remember one situation where two of my colleagues at Aspire Hair & Beauty really didn't hit it off with one another. They were constantly quarrelling and everyone had lost patience with them, but no one wanted to get involved.

Action:

In the end, I decided to take the initiative and act as a sort of mediator to the situation. I was not their manager, so I had to be as tactful as I could so that I wouldn't upset anyone.

I started by explaining that I acknowledged their dislike for each other, and then I drew upon the fact that they are both professionals and can, therefore, put aside their differences for the good of the salon.

Result:

They had a pretty frank discussion, and although I can't say they ended up the best of friends, they did work out an effective strategy for working more productively together.

32 Tell me about a disagreement with a colleague

Evaluation

We all have disagreements with colleagues, but they should never get out of control, or interfere with work.

You may choose to disclose the details of a conflict situation, but make sure it was minor and didn't interfere with work. Subsequently, you may wish to play it safe and declare that while you have had disagreements, they were so minor that you don't really recall the exact details of each. You could then go on to reiterate some examples.

The recruiters want to know that you aren't intimidated by conflicts and have the ability to see things from another person's perspective, and are prepared to use your initiative and interpersonal skills to improve relations with colleagues even in cases where they cannot agree upon certain issues.

Sample Response

Introduction:

Working in a creative environment with other highly skilled professionals, it was natural that we had the occassional clash of ideas, however, any disagreements we did have were so relatively minor and insignificant, I would be hard pressed to recall the exact details.

Situation:

Our disagreements were usually based around our individual preference towards certain products, styles, magazines or equipment.

Action:

Our debates were never confrontational, and they never interfered with our work in any way.

Result:

In fact, some very interesting views emerged from these debates, which sometimes resulted in people, including myself, having a slight change in my perspective, so they were often very educational.

33 Have you successfully worked with a difficult co-worker?

Evaluation

Airlines have a constant rotation of crew onboard each aircraft, and, especially within larger airlines, you may not work with the same crew-members twice. Due to this, it is almost guaranteed that you will encounter a difficult colleague at some stage.

The recruiters want to know that you aren't intimidated by such colleagues or situations, and are prepared to use your initiative to deal with the situation as necessary. You will be assessed on how you approached the colleague and how you dealt with the situation.

Your answer should demonstrate your willingness to co-operate with others to resolve differences, improve relations, and manage conflicts. It should also display your ability to remain patient and positive when challenging situations occur.

Sample Response

Introduction:
If by difficult you mean a person who is constantly complaining, then yes I have.

Situation:
I remember one member of staff was always complaining. Nothing was ever good enough or couldn't possibly work. Everyone had lost patience with her, but because she was so incredibly sensitive, no one said anything.

Action:
I spent some time with her ,and tactfully told her that it appeared as if she was always putting our ideas down.

Result:

On hearing this feedback, she was genuinely horrified at her own behaviour. She explained that she hadn't realised it had made everyone feel that way and agreed that from then on, she would try to be more positive.

Very quickly after that, we saw a change in her behaviour. She became more conscious of her own behaviour and deliberately tried to be more considerate. From that point on, no one could have hoped for a more committed team member.

34 Have you ever worked with someone you disliked?

Evaluation

There will always be someone that we don't like, and to try to convince the recruiter otherwise would not sound honest or credible.

For the most part, this question is asked to determine your ability to get along with other people and manage adversity. The recruiters want to know that you don't allow personal views cause conflict or interfere with work.

The best answer should show that you aren't intimidated or confrontational in such situations, but you put in the commitment necessary to build a respectful and healthy working relationshi

Sample Response

Situation:
Yes, there was one colleague I worked with at Aspire Hair and Beauty that I really found it difficult to like as a person.

Action:
I put my personal views aside, and focused on the skills she brought to the position.

Result:
My personal view of her never changed, and we never became friends, but we did work productively alongside eachother without any problems.

35 Have you had difficulties getting along with colleagues?

Evaluation

No matter how hard we try, or how likeable we are, there will always be someone that we don't hit it off with. To say otherwise, would not sound credible.

For the most part, this question is asked to determine your ability to get along with other people and manage adversity. The recruiters want to know that you don't allow conflict to interfere with work.

The best answer should show that you aren't intimidated or confrontational in such situations, but you put in the commitment necessary to build a respectful and healthy working relationshi

Sample Response

Situation:
I remember one co-worker in particular who flat out didn't like me, it didn't matter what I did or said, or whether I tried to avoid or befriend this person.

Action:
After a couple of days of subtle hostility, I decided to assert myself. I diplomatically explained that I acknowledged her dislike for me, and I asked for input as to what I must do to create a professional relationshi

Result:
Although we never became friends, we were able to maintain more cordial relations thereafter.

36 When have you struggled to fit in?

Evaluation

For the most part, this question may be asked to determine your ability to get along with other people and manage adversity.

The best answer should show that you aren't intimidated or confrontational in such situations, but you put in the commitment necessary to build successful and healthy relationships.

Sample Response

Situation:
When I started working at Aspire Hair & Beauty, I was joining a very close-knit team who had been together for a number of years.

As a result of the number of trainees they had witnessed come and go over the years, they had become displacement, and a little reluctant to accept new starts.

I wouldn't say it was a struggle to fit in as such, but I certainly experienced some growing pains. With remarks such as 'if you are still her then' to contend with, I knew I had to prove myself.

Action:
To show that I was serious about the job, and was not a fly-by-night, I focused a lot of effort on learning my new job. At the same time, I continued to be friendly and respectful of my new colleagues while I made a conscious effort to get to know them.

Result:
As a result of my hard effort, It didn't take long for them to accept me and include me as part of their team. Naturally, I have become closer to some of my colleagues than with others, but we all got on and worked well as a team.

Managing
Adversity...

37 When has your work or idea been criticised?

Evaluation

The recruiter wants to understand how you respond to criticism and deal with authority.

Keep in mind, that everyone experiences criticism from time to time, and to say that you haven't would sound dishonest and naive. Likewise, it doesn't sound very credible to say that you aren't bothered by it either.

The most effective answer is one that shows that you understand that criticism is occasionally part of the professional growth process, and that you are able to use it constructively and learn from it.

Sample Response

Situation:

When I was working at Aspire Hair & Beauty, I had noticed that a lot of our clients wore nail extensions. Excited at the concept, I approached my manager with the suggestion of offering a nail service.

Unfortunately, without doing my homework, I really didn't give her much to go on. Although she was pleased to see that I was enthusiastic about making improvements to the salon, she was, understandably, less than enthusiastic about the idea.

Action:

Convinced that the service would be a success, I decided that further research was necessary if I were to re-approach and convince my manager.

For several weeks thereafter, I approached clients, visited nail bars, approached suppliers, made cost analyses, and even looked into the process of hiring of a nail technician. The feedback from clients, and the results from the research were overwhelmingly positive. From this, I organised my findings into a portfolio, and presented it to my manager.

Result:

Surprised by my findings, she began to re-consider the idea, and over the following couple of months, she carried out her own research.

With the same conclusive results, she embraced the idea, and within a couple of months, the service was added, and a nail technician was hired.

We experienced a dramatic increase in new clientele, and the revenue soon followed. I even got a small bonus in my pay packet for my involvement.

Reflection:

Without solid groundwork, it can be very difficult to put an idea across effectively, thus I learned that adequate research is of paramount importance to success.

38 When have you had to disagree with another person in order to build a positive outcome?

Evaluation

Under certain circumstances, it is important that you are able to voice your disagreement, even if it isn't something that will be popular, or immediately accepted.

The recruiter wants to know that you have the strength of character to voice their concerns and stand up for what you believe in. They also want to be clear that you have the communication and persuasion skills necessary to articulate your disagreement with valid points and well-reasoned arguments, in a logical and reasonable manner.

Your answer should display a patient and positive attitude in dealing with such situations.

Sample Response

Situation:

I remember a client who came to me wanting to have her lovely strawberry blonde hair coloured jet black.

She had uploaded her photo to a virtual hairstyle site, and, because the colour looked good on her photo, she was convinced that jet black was the ideal colour for her.

Action:

I could see by looking at her eyebrows and skin tone that such a drastic colour would completely wash her out. So, sensing that the decision was a disastrous one, and knowing just how difficult it would be to remove such a dense colour, I decided it was in her best interests if I were honest about my opinion.

Determined to have the treatment done, she wouldn't entertain any of my concerns. With this, I went out to my car and fetched several black hair extension pieces. With careful placement, I was able to create an illusion of the result she wanted.

Result:

The client gasped in horror as she turned to see herself in the mirror, and very promptly changed her mind. She couldn't stop thanking me for adverting her away from disaster.

Reflection:

Sometimes, it is in the best interests of the client that you voice your concerns, even if it isn't what the client wants to hear.

39 Describe a time when things were not going well

Evaluation

We all experience down times, and it is how we deal with those times that our true strength of character shows.

Your answer should demonstrate a patient, persistent and positive attitude during challenging times.

Sample Response

Situation:

Shortly after I began freelancing, there was a three day postal strike, and my supplies were seriously delayed. Without the supplies, I couldn't book any appointments, and, regretfully, I had to cancel several appointments as a result.

Action:

I visited several suppliers in the local area, but none had the stock that I needed, and In the end, through fear of losing too much business, I had to travel to my supplier, 118 miles away, to collect duplicate stock.

Result:

This experience made me realise that, although my usual supplier was cheaper than those found locally, it wasn't a long term solution that I could depend upon.

At that early stage, purchasing in bulk wasn't an option I was able to consider, because I lacked adequate finance, and was still learning to anticipate demand.

After considering my options, I determined that a supplier within a reasonable distance was the best long term solution. The following weeks, I visited all the suppliers I could find within a 50 mile radius. I compared stock, carried out quality assessments and weighed up costs. Subsequently, I located on a supplier who was located just 30 miles away. The supplies were slightly more expensive, and it meant changing brands, but I would be within a 40 minute drive of stock if there was an urgent requirement.

Reflection:

Although the experience is not one I would like to repeat, the downtime was minimal, I didn't lose any clients, and it highlighted a problem that, if left unattended, could have created far worse implications later down the line. A blessing in disguise you might say.

Stess
Tolerance...

40 | Tell me about a time when you patience was tested

Evaluation

While it is ok to admit that you feel pressure, those who display a loss of control are certainly not cabin crew material and will not be hired.

Your answer should show that you are well tempered, are able to maintain your composure and remain in control at all times, regardless of the pressure.

Sample Response

Situation:

That's an interesting question because I am, generally speaking, a tolerant person. However, I do remember an incident which occurred shortly after I began freelancing.

I encountered a problem when an associate of mine tried to pressure me into a free hair service based on friendshi

Action:

I proceeded to offer her, what I considered to be, a reasonable discount, but she was not satisfied with my offer, and proceeded to pressure me with emotional blackmail. I remained cordial, but became more assertive as I continued to refuse her demands.

Result:

Rather than accept the reasons for my decision, she became increasingly enraged, and even began to slander my service and friendshi

Shocked at her over-reaction, and concerned about what might develop, I felt I had no option but to withdraw from the situation.

Reflection:

This experience was very challenging, and certainly tested my patience, but I remained calm and, although this particular relationship never recovered, it was a learning experience that, thankfully, hasn't since been repeated.

41 Tell me about a time when you lost your temper

Evaluation

As the sample answer below suggests, losing your temper is counter-productive and inappropriate.

While it is ok to admit that you feel stressed, those who actually lose control of their temper are certainly not cabin crew material and will not be hired.

Consequently, you should explain to the recruiter exactly how and/or why you manage to maintain your composure and keep your temper under control in stressful situations.

You can then follow up with an example of when you demonstrated this ability.

Sample Response

I'm not the kind of person who loses their temper. Losing your temper is counter-productive and inappropriate. By losing your temper, you cannot possibly resolve a problem, you can only make it worse. Even if you're completely right, losing your temper often destroys your ability to convince others that you are right.

My ability to remain calm was clearly demonstrated when an associate of mine became aggressive because I refused to provide a free service to her. Had I retaliated, this situation would have gotten out of control, and who knows what might have happened. Instead, I remained cordial, and eventually withdrew from the situation with no serious consequences.

42

Tell me about a time when you lost control of your emotions

Evaluation

In such a demanding job such as cabin crew, it is important that crew can retain their composure when under pressure.

While it is ok to admit that you feel emotional, those who actually lose control of their emotions are not suitable for the position and will not be hired.

The best way to approach this answer is to explain to the recruiter exactly how and/or why you manage to keep your emotions at bay when you're at work.

Sample Response

I'm not the kind of person who loses control. It is counter-productive and inappropriate, and doesn't gain anything of value.

When I feel stress building, instead of getting emotional, I step back, take a deep breath and begin to focus on the positives. The results are quite dramatic, my whole demeanor changes very rapidly,

I have the power to choose my attitude and control my own thoughts, so I choose to stay in control. From this, I can honestly say that I have never lost control at work.

Traditional Questions...

People Skills (215)

Analytical Skills (221)

Miscellaneous (224)

Wrap it up (228)

Follow-up questions

Recruiters may probe deeper into your answers with follow-up questions. Prepare to be asked:

- What did you learn from the experience?
- What specifically did you say?
- How did you feel?
- Would you do anything differently?
- How did they react?
- What other options did you consider?
- Why did you decide to take the action that you did?
- You mentioned _____. Tell me more about that.
- How did you retain your composure?
- Can you give me an example of that?
- Can you be more specific about _____?

Ice
Breakers...

Tell me about yourself

As you can see from my résumé, I currently work as a freelance hair consultant, and have worked in client-facing roles for the past eight years. During this time, I have worked my way up from a receptionist, to a senior hair stylist within Aspire Hair & Beauty, while simultaneously studying for my NVQ levels 1, 2 and 3.

Now, this brings me to why I am here today, interviewing with you.

I have always wanted to become cabin crew, and, during the course of my career, I have been gradually mastering the skills needed to perform its tasks. Specifically, I have fine tuned my interpersonal and communication skils, and have developed outstanding customer care skills. I'm confident that these skillls, combined with my friendly and positive nature, will compliment your existing team and enable me to deliver the standard of service that passengers have come to expect from Aspire Airlines.

I'd now like to discuss how I might continue my success by joining your team.

Would you like something to drink?

If drinks are in the room already, then say "yes please" and have one if you want.

If drinks are not in the room, say "if you are having one, I'll join you, but otherwise I'm fine, thank you".

How was your journey?

There were no problems. Your map was a great hel

Personal Growth & Development...

Education...

Do you feel your education and training prepared you well for the challenges in the work force?

Absolutely. To achieve good results at school I had to work hard, set my goals, and do my best to achieve them. The same principles apply in the work force. The problem-solving and goal-setting skills that I acquired have helped me a lot throughout my career.

Do you think new employers should consider grades?

Of course, an employer should take everything into consideration, and along with grades will be an evaluation of willingness and manageability, an understanding of how business works, and actual work experience. Combined, such experience and professional skills can be more valuable than grades alone.

Why didn't you stay on at school or continue full time education?

I wanted to continue full time education, but personal circumstances meant that I needed to earn a living rather than run up debts studying. Everything worked out well in the end, though, because I managed to educate myself alongside my work.

Why didn't you do better in your exams?

My results were above average. If I could do it again, my grades would be much higher. I'd not only work harder, but I've also learned a lot since then.

What subjects were the easiest for you?

I wouldn't say that any of the subjects were easy, as they all required hard work. However, because I have a natural creative ability, art and design was the one I found to be the least difficult. I felt a great deal of pleasure from those lessons, and my exam results reflected this.

What subjects gave you the most difficulty?

I never had a great deal of knowledge about science, but I forced myself to study hard so I managed to achieve above average results.

I see you studied French at school, what is your fluency?

I'm not as fluent as I once was. I would welcome the opportunity to increase my fluency.

Self Development...

What is your opinion of the importance of training and development?

Effective training and development are absolutely necessary in order to improve efficiency and readiness for the work force.

How have you changed in the last five years?

I feel like I have matured, rather than aged, five years. The skills I have acquired and the qualities I have developed have changed me enormously, and I know there are parts of me that are still not being utilised half as effectively as they could be.

What are the three most important skills that you have developed in your career so far?

Through working with colleagues, dealing with suppliers and customers, I've significantly improved my social and communication skills. Second, I've developed my problem solving skills, and as for number three, I've greatly enhanced my people management and leadership skills.

Each of these will transfer well and benefit my performance as a cabin crew member.

What have you learned from your work experience?

There are three general things I have learned from past experience. First, it's better to ask a dumb question than make a stupid mistake. Second, it's better to promise less and produce more than to make unrealistic forecasts. Finally, I have learned that what is good for the company is good for me.

What do you do to improve yourself?

Since leaving school, I don't think a day has passed that I didn't improve myself to some extent.

I utilise every available opportunity to expand my knowledge and acquire further skills. I educate myself informally through reading journals and self help books, so I have continued to learn and grow.

Alongside the on-the-job training I received at Aspire Hair & Beauty, I studied part time to achieve my NVQ levels 1, 2 and 3 in hairdressing. Following completion of my training, I took it upon myself to complete a creative cutting course.

Career Focus & Direction...

Work History...

What do you like about your current job?

I like everything about my current job. I don't think I'd be able to really excel if I weren't truly interested in the work, or if I were merely motivated by its financial rewards.

Rather than pick out little details of the routine work, here are three general things. First is customer satisfaction: seeing the clients face glow with happiness when their hair has been transformed, it's very satisfying and drives me to do better. Second, I like constant interaction with people as it has enabled me to strengthen my communication and social ability. Finally, I enjoy being creative with hair and finding new ways to please the customer.

What have you enjoyed most about your current job?

I enjoy the feeling of pride when I say goodbye to another satisfied client. Seeing their face glow with happiness when there is transformed is very satisfying.

What do you dislike about your current job?

I really like this work, so I honestly can't think of any major dislikes. I guess my answer will have to come under the category or nuisances.

The biggest nuisance is the paperwork that seems to slow down the action. I realise the importance of documentation, and I cooperatively fill out the forms, but I'm always looking for efficiencies in that area that will get me out in front of the customer where I belong.

What have you enjoyed least about your current job?

It is exciting working freelance, and I have built up a substantial base of satisfied customers, however, the drawback to working freelance is the lack of security. I don't know what the future holds and sometimes that is a frightening concept.

Although no job is secure nowadays, I would prefer to have a situation where I can follow a clear career path. I think even more significantly, though, I actually miss working with other people and having colleagues to share ideas with. I like working in a team environment.

Which particular aspect of your work do you find most frustrating?

That's an interesting question because I am, generally speaking, a tolerant person. However, slow periods can be sources of frustration, but at times like that I put more effort into advertising and establishing new clientele. That way, the slow period's don't last long.

Which position gave you the most satisfaction?

It's hard to pick a single favourite position because there have been aspects of every position that I've enjoyed, each for different reasons.

However, my most satisfying job to date has been my current one because it offers me the opportunity to use all of my initiative and skill to solve problems and get things done, whilst providing similar tasks to that in my previous positions.

Which position would you say was the most boring?

I haven't found any of the work in my career boring. I've always been too busy to be bored. There has been something interesting, something that held my attention, about every position I've held.

Which position did you least enjoy?

Each position had its different challenges, and required me to utilise my knowledge, skills and experience to meet those challenges. This made my working environment stimulating and provided opportunities to develop in many ways. So I cannot really say what position I least enjoyed as each working experience was valuable.

How do you maintain your interest in your work?

Quite easily. When I see the clients face glow with happiness when their hair is transformed, it's very satisfying and makes the hard work worth it. Also, because no two clients are the same and each requires something different, this makes the work much more interesting as I am able to utilise my creative ability.

Why are you dissatisfied with your current job?

I'm not dissatisfied with my job, in many ways I am very happy where I am. I'm not looking around actively, but there are only so many extraordinary opportunities that come along in this life and this is one of them. This job calls for the skills I have and offers the scope I want.

Have you worked on night shifts before?

So far, I haven't worked on a night shift. However, I have often worked long hours and late shifts, so I could work a night shift without any problems.

When have you worked unsociable hours?

Working freelance can involve working unsociable hours during the busy periods. During these peak times, it is quite common for me to be working through the day, right into the late evening, typically 12 - 13 hours.

Is there a lot of pressure in your current work?

Working freelance carries a degree of pressure that I find stimulating, and enjoy working with. When I first started freelance, I experienced the pressures of being my own boss, while I was also learning to successfully run my new business.

Since then, my business and my experience has grown, and the pressure I experience now is due to the shear size of my client base. Because of demand, I experience a lot of time restrictions. In between carrying out the services, I sometimes find it difficult to make time to complete paperwork, hold consultations and collect supplies. There are times when I have to call upon family and friends just to help relieve the workload.

Fortunately, I am a self starter and am good at working on my own initiative.

What have been the biggest frustrations in your career?

I've always approached my career with enthusiasm, so I really haven't experienced much frustration. When I do find myself up against a source of frustration, such as when clients miss appointments, or supplies are delayed, I try to convert it into a learning experience and an opportunity to make improvements.

What has been the biggest disappointment of your career?

I couldn't say that I have had any big disappointments in my career. I have been doing the type of work I like, and that makes good use of my knowledge and experience. However, I was a little let down when I didn't get onto a part time hairdressing course after leaving school, and yet I ended up enjoying myself and doing well anyway.

Naturally, if I don't get this job, it will be my biggest disappointment because it is something I really want.

Have you done the best work you are capable of?

That's hard to say, because I'm always striving to do better, but in doing so I increase my skills and, therefore, always see room for improvement. I have had some great accomplishments in my career, such as my success at working freelance, but I believe the best is yet to come.

What has been the most significant accomplishment/ achievement up to this point in your career?

Although I believe my biggest accomplishments are still ahead of me, I feel my most significant accomplishment to date was rising from the receptionist and general hand to become a hairdresser. I think it demonstrates not only my growth, but also the confidence my manager had in my ability. I have accomplished many things in my career since, but I still look back on that one event as the turning point and the accomplishment that made all the others possible.

What was the least enjoyable experience in your work experience?

I cannot recall one particular moment or situation in my work history that I can say was the least enjoyable, mainly because I've always approached my career with a positive and enthusiastic attitude. When unfavourable situations occur, I see them as challenges and opportunities to learn.

What was the most enjoyable experience in your work experience?

My most enjoyable experiences are usually a result of satisfied customers. I get a sense of happiness in making people happy. That feeling of pride when you see the clients face glow with happiness when their hair has been transformed, it's very satisfying and makes me proud to see what I have done.

In what areas of your current work are you strongest?

I am sure it is dealing with people. My interpersonal skills are very good, and I pride myself on being able to build rapport quickly with new people. I think my professional attitude and common sense approach goes down well with clients, and I have always received positive feedback with regards to follow through.

Additionally, I am good at what I do. I have a natural flair for design, good judgement, and am good at coming up with new ideas.

On top of those reasons, I am really enthusiastic about my work, and I put a great deal of energy into it.

In what areas of your current work are you weakest?

I don't have any major weaknesses that interfere with how I do my job. The only area which can always be improved is the way to run a successful business. I have gained a great deal of business knowledge and experience during my freelancing career, such as time management, problem solving, book keeping, etc, but I feel that you can never be too good or should ever stop trying to polish your business skills.

Career Progression...

Why have you decided to change professions at this stage of your career?

This career turnaround hasn't come suddenly. I have always liked this profession and have been gradually mastering the skills needed to perform its tasks. I have reached a point where I am prepared to assume the responsibility.

Why did you stay with the same employer for so long?

I was there for several years, but in a variety of different roles so it felt as though I was undergoing frequent changes without actually changing employer.

Why were you fired/dismissed?

Example 1
I was desperate for work and took the job without fully understanding the expectations. It turned out that my competencies were not a right match for the employer's needs, and so we agreed that it was time for me to move on to a position that would be more suitable. It's not a mistake I have ever repeated.

Example 2
I survived the first downsizing, but unfortunately this one got me.

Example 3
Unfortunately I had been going through a rough patch in my personal life which, although has now been solved, upset my work life.

Example 4
Being dismissed was a blessing in disguise as it made me realise that I'd wanted my career to move in a different direction and had been letting this interfere with my work. I realize I should have taken control and done some things differently, but I'm a lot wiser now.

Why did you leave your last job?

While I did enjoy working for Aspire Hair & Beauty, and appreciate the skills I developed while I was with the salon, I felt I was not being challenged enough in the job, and, after working my way up through the salon, there were no further opportunities for advancement.

Why do you want to leave your current job?

Being cabin crew is something I have always wanted to do, and I am now at a point in my life where I am prepared to make the career and lifestyle change. I want to take advantage of that opportunity.

How do you feel about your career progress to date?

In looking back over my career, I am very satisfied with my progress, I have achieved all that I have set myself, and more. I have identified opportunities that would stretch and develop me, and have been pleased with my achievements. I have gained a great deal in terms of knowledge and experience, and I am now seeking to maintain this momentum.

If you could start your career over again, what would you do differently?

I don't regret the course of my career, because I have worked for an interesting company, with extraordinary people. I have learnt from their advice, to better myself and ultimately, I have succeeded in my chosen profession. I now look forward to progressing further.

Where do you picture yourself in five years?

This is a lively and expanding company by all accounts, so I very much hope that I shall be here in five years time. My job will have increased at least one possibly two levels in responsibility and scope, and I'll have become a thorough professional with a clear understanding of the industry and airline. I'll have made a significant contribution and will be working on new ways to further my career.

What is your idea of success?

Success for me is about knowing that I have made a difference both to myself and my organisation. I like to make a difference to myself by developing my own skills, and I like to make a difference to my organisation by achieving good results.

Describe a time when you thought you were doing well

I am happy with the way things are going now. I have achieved everything I have set myself and more, and hopefully I am looking forward to an exciting new career as a cabin crew member with Aspire airline.

Why do you think you have succeeded at working freelance?

No two clients are alike, and I feel that my secret to my success is making them feel that they get individual service created for their individual needs. Second, I place strong emphasis on quality, so my work is consistently exceptional. This, combined with my reasonable prices, has enabled me to increase my customer base dramatically.

Finally, I have worked hard to build loyal relationships with my customers, and that has certainly helped translate my business into success.

Cabin
Crew...

Knowledge About the Job..

What do you think the role of cabin crew involves?

Cabin crew are on board an aircraft for safety reasons. When things go wrong, whether there is a medical emergency, a fire break-out, a terrorism threat, a violent passenger or mechanical failure, the cabin crew is there to take action. This may involve directing passengers during an evacuation, controlling a drunken passenger or administering first aid.

Between boarding and disembarkment, crew will generally spend most of their time tending to passenger comfort. While meal and beverage services play a large part of a crew's duties, their responsibilities will be as diverse as the needs of the passengers, and they generally spend much of the flight on their feet tending to those needs.

Behind the scenes, there is also the cleaning and preparation of the aircraft between flights, the completion of paperwork, stock checks and replenishment, and safety procedures to complete.

All the while, they are expected to deliver the highest standards of customer care, appearing friendly and approachable to every passenger.

Clearly, the profession is a very demanding one, but it is also a very exciting and fulfilling one for those who have the necessary qualities, which I believe I do have.

What do you think are the advantages of the position?

Clearly, the profession is a very demanding one, but it is also a very exciting and fulfilling one, with opportunities to visit places and experience cultures that are beyond most people's reach.

Plus, the sheer dynamics of different crew, passenger profiles, destinations and roster structures ensure that there will always be variety.

It's a job I will find very rewarding in a number of ways.

What do you think are the disadvantages of this position?

Cabin crew experience flight delays and cancellations just as passengers do. This makes for very long and tiring shifts, irregular working patterns and unpredictable schedules.

In addition, regularly crossing different time zones can cause jet lag and lead to disturbed sleep patterns and fatigue.

Ultimately, the role is a very physically and mentally demanding one, but it is also a very exciting and fulfilling one. I look forward to the challenges the role provides.

What would you change about this position?

I relish the challenges that this position will provide and there's nothing I've seen that intimidates me in any way. By applying for this position, I have accepted everything that comes with it and therefore I would not change anything.

Do you think the role of cabin crew is glamorous?

Having thoroughly researched the position, I am aware that the glamour, that is often mistakenly associated with the role, is rather superficial.

Working as cabin crew is much more complex than it appears on the surface. Sure there are benefits of travel, and the crew certainly do make themselves appear glamorous, but the constant traveling between time zones, the long and tiring shifts, irregular working patterns and unpredictable schedules make the profession an exhausting one that places tough demands on social and family life.

Therefore, no, I don't view the position of cabin crew as a glamorous role, but rather a challenging one, and I do like a good challenge.

What qualities do you think a good cabin crew member should have?

Passengers generally spend more time with the cabin crew than with any other members of the airline staff, so they have a vital role in giving a good impression of the airline as a whole. This means cabin crew members need to have good communication and customer care skills, and display desirable traits such as sincerity, a spirit of enthusiasm, confidence and a sense of humour.

They must be totally flexible about working with new people, flying different routes and working unsociable hours. They may deal with money, including foreign currency, so they should be honest as well as confident with numbers. Team working skills are also very important as is being fairly self contained, and satisfied in your own company.

The ability to manage change and adversity is another necessary quality for cabin crew. They should be able to show that they have the strength of character to cope, which means approaching difficult and emergency situations in a calm and objective way – and being polite yet resolute in handling an abrasive customer.

These are all attributes that I possess and are the primary reasons why I will make an excellent member of cabin crew.

What sort of individual do you think we are looking for?

I believe you are looking for an individual who has good communication, teamwork, and customer care skills, and displays desirable traits such as maturity, friendliness, approachability and a sense of humour. The successful candidate would also need to have the ability to remain calm and level headed in emergency situations and be totally flexible about working with new people, flying different routes and working unsociable hours.

Do you know anything about cabin crew training?

The training lasts for five weeks, and the subjects that are covered include: Safety and emergency procedures, such as fire fighting, first aid, security and hijack procedures, and crowd control. Also covered is dealing with passengers, foreign currency and personal grooming and deportment. This initial period is followed by further on-the-job training, and usually a period of regular on board assessment.

What aspects of customer service are most important to our passengers?

People will return to a favourite airline not merely because the price, destinations, in-flight entertainment, and food is good. Equally differential in their choice is the standard of service.

Passengers want to feel welcome, while being looked after, whatever their needs, by people who are friendly, polite, approachable, willing to listen and professional, whatever the time of day and whatever the pressure.

What do you think is the main cause of some passenger's frustrations?

Common causes of irritation for passengers include flight delays, lost luggage, inadequate catering facilities and lack of space. Other causes may include incorrect, poorly displayed or missing information and poor service.

Why do you think some passengers take out their frustrations on cabin crew?

Cabin crew wear the airline's uniform. They are, therefore, considered a representative which makes them an easy target for passengers to vent their frustrations upon.

Suitability For the Job...

Why should we hire you instead of someone with cabin crew experience?

Although I might not have cabin crew experience, I have the necessary skills to make an impressive start, and the willingness to learn and improve. Sometimes employers do better when they hire people who don't have a great deal of repetitive experience. That way, they can train these employees in their methods and ways of doing the job. Training is much easier than un-training.

Why should we hire you rather than another applicant?

I can't tell you why you should hire me instead of another candidate, but I can tell you why you should hire me.

Why should we hire you?

This job is exactly what I'm looking for, and I'm exactly what you are wanting. My skills and experience closely match the major requirements and diverse responsibilities for this role. Plus I will bring a depth of practical knowledge and experience that will transfer well and benefit my performance as a cabin crew member, such as handling customer service issues, sales, working under pressure and communicating with different types of people.

Furthermore, I am an honest and upright person who understands the need for high standards and rules, and I refuse to compromise on standards and integrity. Within this, I can be relied upon to put the customer first, and will always consider the needs of colleagues and of the airline.

I'm driven to achieve, to surpass my most recent record, so you'll never see me deliver merely acceptable performance. I keep calm and don't let attention to detail slip when there is a lot of pressure, and can be relied on to pull with the team when it's facing any kind of challenge.

I really think that the airline could use someone with my attributes. Aspire Airlines provide a fine service, and I can offer top professionalism. Together we will make a winning team.

What contribution can you make to ensure passengers will fly with us again?

My friendly and positive nature, along with excellent customer care skills will enable me to deliver the standard of service that will make passengers feel welcome, valued and relaxed.

What qualities do you have that would make you a good member of cabin crew?

My skills and experience closely match the major requirements and diverse responsibilities for this role. Plus I will bring a depth of practical knowledge and experience that will transfer well and benefit my performance as a cabin crew member.

I am used to working under pressure, and I thrive on the challenges that these situations create.

Furthermore, I am an experienced team player who always work hard to support and contribute towards the overall team goal for success. I am a people person, and would consistently deliver excellent customer service to passengers of all levels. I'm driven to achieve, to surpass my most recent record, so you'll never see me deliver merely acceptable performance.

I feel that my personal qualities, along with the skills and experience I have gained from working in client-facing roles for the past eight years would make me an excellent member of cabin crew.

How has your work experience prepared you for the role?

My work experience closely matches the requirements and diverse responsibilities of this position in many ways. Working as a hairdresser I interact with a range of people daily and have to handle responsibility with a minimum of supervision. I am responsible for establishing and maintaining relationships with clients, dealing with customer service issues, sales, and admin.

Furthermore, I am required to stand for long periods, work unsociable hours, pay attention to detail and be self starting with a lot of mental discipline.

I feel my experience will transfer well and enable me to make a significant contribution to this position. Combined with the training I will receive, I believe I will make an outstanding employee.

I'm not sure you are suitable for the position. Convince me.

I am absolutely suitable. In fact, I am confident that I am perfect for this position.

You are looking for someone with excellent customer care skills. Well, as you can see from my résumé, I have worked in client-facing roles for eight years, so have had plenty of experience dealing with the various aspects. I also run a successful business that relies on customer satisfaction. The fact that I am still in business, and have a solid client base, which continues to grow, is a clear testament to my abilities.

Furthermore, you also need someone who has a calm approach, and retains their composure in the face of adversity. Again, I have certainly demonstrated this capability on several occasions throughout my career. Specifically, there was an occurrence when an associate of mine became aggressive because I had refused to provide a free service to her. Had I retaliated or become angry, this situation would have gone out of control, and who knows what might have happened. Instead, I remained cordial, and eventually withdrew from the situation with no serious consequences.

Beyond these things, I have a friendly and positive nature, I am hardworking, and I will always strive to deliver the same high standard of service that passengers have come to expect from Aspire Airlines.

I am confident that my skills, experience and personal qualities combined will compliment your existing team and allow me to make a positive contribution to the airline's ongoing success.

Aren't you overqualified for this position?

As you note, I've worked at a higher level, but I wouldn't say that I am overqualified, but fully qualified. With more than the minimal experience, I offer immediate returns on your investment. Don't you want a winner with the skill sets and attitudes to do just that?

Do you think your lack of language skills will affect your ability to perform the job?

I admit my language skills are a little light, however, should I be offered the position, I would be sure to work on increasing my language abilities further.

Do you feel ready for a more responsible position?

As I manage a business with real success, I have certainly demonstrated that I can manage responsibility. I believe that eight years experience working closely with customers, has prepared me professionally and personally to move up to this role. My customer care and teamwork skills have been finely tuned over the years, and I know I am capable of greater achievements.

Do you feel confident in your ability to handle this position?

Yes, absolutely. I'm very confident in my abilities. I'm familiar with the basic job requirements and I learn quickly. It undoubtedly will take time and effort on my part, but I'm more than willing to devote that time and effort.

What makes this job different from the ones you have held?

I really don't believe that any two jobs are exactly the same. Different customers, different projects and different approaches make every job unique. There are, however, more similarities than differences, and if I focus on those similarities rather than the differences I will accomplish more and be contributing right from the start.

What qualities/experience do you not presently have?

From what I know about the position, I seem to have all the skills and experience required to make a thorough success. I don't believe that there are any areas that indicate gaps in my ability to do this job well and any gaps that may exist will be presented and filled during the initial training.

Will you be able to cope with the change in environment?

Definitely. I welcome the challenge of learning about and adapting to a new environment, that's one of the reasons I'm seeking to make a career change right now. Any major change, while always containing some challenge is a chance to grow, learn, and advance.

How will you adapt your behaviour to the wide range of ethnic differences you will encounter on the job?

Due to various perceptions of meanings, and ease of misunderstandings. I will be careful in my use of body language and hand gestures.

In the case of a language barrier, I will try to ensure that the passenger understands my style of speech, pace, vocabulary or accent, by speaking slightly slower than usual, using clearer pronunciations, and avoiding slang, jargon, buzzwords and clichés. To further ensure comprehension, I will also make additional use of facial expressions and hand gestures where appropriate.

If at any time I feel that the passenger has not understood, I will spend a little time to discuss it with them.

If I am offered the position, I will also take steps towards enhancing my language skills, which will allow further flexibility.

How do you feel about the routine tasks and irregular hours of this job?

I accept that every role carries with it a certain amount of routine in order to get the job done. If my job involves repetitive work, it is my responsibility to carry it out to the best of my abilities. As for irregular hours I would expect to have an indication of my core hours, but will work the hours that are necessary in order to fulfill the requirements of the role.

How do you feel about working at Christmas, and other special occasions?

I understand this from your job description, and I considered this carefully before I applied, so it would not be a problem.

Wouldn't you miss spending time with your family and friends when you are required to work on special occasions?

Naturally, I would miss spending time with my friends and family, but my career is important to me and my family and friends respect and appreciate that fact.

How do you feel about living out of a suitcase?

I have no concerns.

How do you feel about a formal dress code?

I have always liked to dress formally and feel very comfortable wearing formal attire. I realise that a standard of dress is necessary in order to project a professional image to the passengers.

How will you cope with the wide range of personalities among our employees?

The same way I have coped in the past. Working at Aspire Hair & Beauty, I worked with people who had very different personalities. Some of them had loud and exuberant personalities, whilst others were sensitive and quiet. I understand that a range of personalities exist in any workplace, and I observe and respect each of them accordingly.

How do you feel about working in a very multi-cultural environment, colleagues and customers?

I learnt about different cultures, customs and religions from a young age, through my years of education at school. I also have a cosmopolitan group of friends, so I feel comfortable with people who are from other ethnic backgrounds.

Aspire Hair & Beauty specialised in Afro Caribbean hairdressing and, therefore, attracted a large variety of people from many ethnic backgrounds. The manager and supervisor were both originally from Jamaica and spoke English as a second language. Not only did I have a good working relationship with them, we also became good friends.

This is a long hours culture, is that a problem for you?

I understand that this a demanding job, but I really do thrive on the challenge of this sort of work and have worked long hours in the past, so I am willing to work whatever hours are necessary to get the work done.

What will you look forward to most in this job?

I look forward to having the opportunity to build a career with a reputable airline that I use, and have grown to trust. The chance to apply my skills, in a job that I enjoy, and where I am sufficiently challenged to develop further.

I am confident that I will be successful as cabin crew and would make a positive contribution to the position, and the airline's ongoing success.

What challenges do you look forward to?

An opportunity to apply my interpersonal skills in a new team, with a different set of customers, in a new environment.

Why do you want to become cabin crew?

Because this job is tailored to my core competencies, which includes excellent people skills and the ability to remain calm under pressure, I am confident that I will be good at the job.

My friendly and positive nature will enable me to fit right in and compliment your existing team, and I could use the customer care skills I have developed over the course of my career to deliver the standard of service that passengers have come to expect from Aspire Airlines.

I feel that, for the above reasons, I would be successful as cabin crew and would make a positive contribution to the position, and the airline.

How will this job help you reach your career goals?

I am consistently striving to increase my knowledge and skills, and I believe that this position can offer me a real step up in terms of challenge and experience. I feel that my present career plans would be more than fulfilled by this role. The position would allow me to use the skills I already have, but be sufficiently challenging to give the opportunity for further development.

This position requires long hours. Will this be a problem for your family life?

My career plays an important part of my life. My family and friends realise and appreciate the fact and are very flexible with my schedule. They support me 100%.

Knowledge About the Airline...

Why do you want to work for this airline?

I have viewed your website, and can see this is an airline with solid foundations and excellent values. Also, I'm a frequent flyer with Aspire Airlines, and I like the idea of working for a reputable airline whose services I already use and trust.

The service I receive onboard is always fantastic, and I'm confident that my friendly and positive nature will enable me to fit right in and compliment your existing team.

I'm positive that my extensive background and experience in customer service roles, along with my excellent people skills, will enable me to make a positive contribution to the airline's ongoing success.

What do you know about this airline?

The airline began operations in February 1980 with one leased aircraft, serving two destinations to New York and Los Angeles.

The airline now serves 67 destinations in 54 countries worldwide. Three new routes: Birmingham, Dubai and Sao Paulo is being added to the network in 2009 with plans for another 25-50 destinations before 2015.

The airline has acquired more than 300 international awards for customer service and is among the world's most profitable airlines.

Have you ever flown with us? What do you think about the way we run our operation?

I had the opportunity to fly with Aspire Airlines from London to Los Angeles in October 2004.

Onboard, the service was excellent, and I felt like I was flying first class. The meal was outstanding, the seats were comfortable, and the variety of entertainment was impressive.

The crew were attentive, competent and very friendly to talk to. They certainly made the flight a pleasant and comfortable one.

How would you rate us against our competitors?

Example 1
It's so difficult to be objective, and I really don't like to slight your competition.

Example 2
My experiences with each of the airlines I have flown with have all been good, and I never had a problem or cause for complaint, however, an advantage of Aspire Airlines is the crew. They really take care of all their passengers and do everything to make the flight as pleasant as possible. They are attentive, competent and very friendly.

Do you think we have a good reputation?

During my research into your airline, I did not come across any information that indicated a bad reputation. In fact, quite the contrary, you seem to have a very good reputation.

What is the worst thing you have heard about us?

The worst thing I have heard about Aspire Airlines is that competition for jobs is fierce because it is a terrific airline. Everything else I have heard, have been overly positive.

Is there anything you think we do badly?

I haven't come across anything to suggest that you are doing anything badly, in fact, quite the opposite. Plus I am sure you wouldn't enjoy your current success if you were doing anything really wrong, and I wouldn't be applying to join you if that were the case.

Miscellaneous...

How long would you stay with us?

I'm a loyal sort of person, and am approaching this job with a long-term view. If the job is as challenging as I'm sure it is, and the opportunities for development within your organisation are as good as I believe they are, I would like to think that I can make a positive contribution to Aspire Airlines for the foreseeable future.

If you were to leave the flight department, where would you turn your skills?

If for any reason I were to leave the flight department, I would turn my skills to cabin crew training, recruitment, or possibly airport personnel.

What do you hope to achieve from this position?

I hope to build a long term career with this airline, grow and develop within the position, and make a positive contribution to the airline's continued success.

How did you become interested in the position of cabin crew?

Living close to Aspire Airport, my passion for flying started at a very young age. It wasn't until I carried out a career suitability test at school, though, that I really started to consider cabin crew as a serious future prospect.

The test examined personal attributes, goals and skills, and the result came back suggesting suitability for the occupation. Based on this, I did a little more research into the job and agreed, this seems to be a job for which I am suited, and is one I will feel committed to.

This position will involve relocating, how will you adjust to the different lifestyle?

I realise that this position involves transfers, and I bore that in mind when I applied. I am fully aware of what to expect from the research I have done and would welcome the different lifestyle.

Have you applied to any other airlines?

I have researched other airlines that would interest me, but after researching the history, development and future plans of Aspire Airlines, along with meeting people who work here, it seems like a perfect fit. I really appreciate what Aspire has to offer in the way of growth potential and good reputation, and I would really like to work for you. So although it is taking a bit of a risk, I wanted to see how things went with my application to you, before I considered applying to any other airlines.

What do you look for in a potential employer?

Making a job change is a major decision, a long term commitment that I take very seriously. I, therefore, I look for a good reputation in an active, creative and stimulating environment where I am limited only by my capabilities and where positive results are acknowledged. I believe Aspire Airlines offers all of this and more.

How do you research the companies you wish to work for?

First, I visit the company's website where I can learn more about its values and future plans. Here I can also learn more about the position, its responsibilities and potential for growth. I then search the internet to find out about its reputation, and may even make a personal visit to the company's premises where I can talk to employees and assess the overall environment.

Have you applied for any other jobs?

At this stage, the position of cabin crew is the only position of interest that fits both my skills and career aspirations.

How do you feel about looking for another job?

Looking for another job is an opportunity. I don't need to look for another job, I do it so that I can continue to grow professionally.

Would you like to have my job?

Only for the next ten minutes so that I could hire myself.

Character...

Your Views

How would you describe yourself?

My work has shown me to be a very ambitious, hardworking and professional individual who readily adapts to new people and work environments. I am enthusiastic about taking up new challenges, I have a natural desire to learn, and am forever the optimist,

Personally, I am a funloving and approachable person, whom others consider as sincere and friendly.

If you had to characterise yourself in one sentence, what would you say?

I am a funloving and approachable person, who is ambitious, hardworking and enthusiastic.

Rate yourself on a scale from 1 to 10

I would rate myself as an 8. I always give my best, but in doing so I increase my skills. I, therefore, always see room for improvement.

What makes you stand out from the crowd?

My flexibility certainly makes me stand out. I readily adapt to new environments and people, I am able to alter my perspective in the face of adversity, I am a self starter so am able to work well on my own initiative, or I can work efficiently as port of a team.

Would you classify yourself as a hard-working or relatively laid back?

When I'm at work, I always give my best and try to achieve as much as possible. I have always been self-motivated, and not to work hard would be against my character.

Are you an introvert or extrovert?

I am quite an extrovert, but I'm not so dependent upon other people that I get withdrawal symptoms when left alone.

What is your biggest weakness?

I tend to spend longer than necessary making sure that things are perfect, and sometimes get a little frustrated if I don't achieve excellence.

I did learn early on in my career that this slows output, but on the other hand, without such attention to detail the consistency and accuracy of my work could be affected. It is a difficult balancing act but I am working on finding a more balanced approach.

What are your best qualities?

My friendly and positive attitude are qualities that certainly define me as a person. I also have very good interpersonal skills and am able to build rapport quickly with new people. In fact, at Aspire Hair & Beauty, I was often asked to carry out the shampoo because the manager knew I would make the clients feel welcome and important.

What is your greatest strength?

I have very good interpersonal skills, and I pride myself on being able to build rapport quickly with new people. To me, establishing rapport seems to be a natural tendency. In fact, at Aspire Hair & Beauty, I was often asked to carry out the shampoo because the manager knew I would make the clients feel welcome and important.

Are you a self-starter?

Absolutely. I rarely need others to motivate me, as I am very directed by my own career and am the sort of person who enjoys taking the initiative.

For example, when I began working at Aspire Hair & Beauty, the inventory system was outdated, and the storage room was very messy and disorganised. I came in on my day off, cleaned up the mess, organised the store cupboards, and catalogued it all on the new inventory forms. Thereafter when orders arrived, it was easy to organise and, therefore, retrieve.

If I'm able to do the task, instead of waiting for the job to be done, I simply do it.

Do you consider yourself assertive or aggressive?

Definitely assertive. When I think of an aggressive person, I think of someone who bullies and attacks others to get his or her way. Being assertive, on the other hand, allows me to make my ideas known without disparaging the ideas and opinions of others.

What characteristics are necessary for success working freelance?

Working freelance, you have to be a self starter, able to spot opportunities, and act on your own initiative without the support of others.

It requires the friendly nature of someone who is able to talk to customers easily and anticipate their needs. You'll also need to be self sufficient as you'll need to find innovative ways to get around various challenges that business life will throw at you.

What characteristics are necessary for success in your current job?

As it is a personal service in which the customer's satisfaction is the key to success, you need to be friendly, polite and able to talk to customers easily. You should work quickly and well with your hands, doing detailed work, and have a creative, artistic sense.

Self-presentation is important, so you should also be well groomed. You also need to be fit and able to stand for long periods.

Other People's Views

How would a friend describe you?

They would say I am easy to get on with, have a good sense of humour, am outgoing, and generally cheerful. They would also say I am someone who keeps personal commitments and protects personal confidences.

How would an enemy describe your character?

I suppose they might say that I am tenacious, brave, and driven.

Why Tenacious
I am certainly not a person to give in without a struggle, but on the other hand, I'm quite realistic about my limits.

Why Brave
I am prepared to confront issues when there is a need, and I'm not too concerned, but I weigh the consequences and don't act irresponsibly.

Why Driven
I know how to push for what I want, but can back off when it is advisable to do so.

What would colleagues say about you?

Judging by the successful and professional relationship I had with my colleagues, I would expect to be portrayed as hard working, motivated, a good communicator and a person of high integrity and moral. I believe they would also tell you that I am easy to get on with and am usually cheerful.

What aspects of your personality would your colleagues be less enthusiastic about?

Because I am always optimistic, and never air my grievances or have my emotions on public display, unfortunately, this can be difficult for some people to understand.

For example, in the early days of working at Aspire Hair & Beauty, before my colleagues got to know me, they took it as a lack of consideration or care when they were feeling the pressure of a situation, and were not feeling so positive. They soon got to know me, though, and I like to think that my positive nature had a positive influence on them.

What would superiors say are your strengths?

My superiors always rated my job performance well, formally and informally. In fact, I was always rated as being capable of accepting further responsibilities.

I received particularly favourable evaluations in the areas of customer care and working with co workers.

I also received high ratings in the area of initiative and enthusiasm. Because I look at each situation as a potentially exciting challenge, my superior's say I create excitement in other team members, which results in a greater team effort and higher output.

What did superiors think are your weaknesses?

What might be perceived by some as weaknesses, are really my strengths. For example, I occasionally received comments about putting in too many hours. They said that they thought I might be over-exerting myself, and may burn myself out.

I see it as dedication and enthusiasm for my career, and I personally don't feel I over-exert myself. Outside of work, I take time to relax and regularly go swimming, and practice yoga routines. This gives me a break from the work environment and keeps me stimulated.

Stress Tolerance

What types of people annoy you or try your patience?

That's an interesting question, because I am a very tolerant person. However, I am only human, and there are instances where my patience is put to the test. However, I am able to control myself and my emotions, so I never let my patience move beyond the testing stage.

We all have control over our emotions and our actions, I choose to remain in control.

Do you have difficulties tolerating people with different views or interests than you?

No. I recognise that everyone has their own views, and that they may not always correspond with my own. Differing views and personalities are what makes us individual, so I don't let other people's views or interests affect how I feel about them.

How do you manage stress?

I always take time at the end of the day to reflect upon the day's events and to analyse what I could have done better. When I notice prolonged problems, I take action to bring about change. I have found that taking time to reflect is a key element to managing stress.

Furthermore, I practice stress management through relaxation, rest and regular exercise, which helps me to unwind. I also avoid substances that can negatively affect my good health, such as cigarettes, alcohol and fast food.

How often do you lose your temper?

I am patient, understanding, and easy to deal with and never lose my temper. I regard that sort of behaviour as counterproductive and inappropriate. By losing your temper, you cannot possibly resolve a problem: you can only make it worse. Even if you're completely right, losing your temper often destroys your ability to convince others that you are right.

What makes you angry or impatient?

Anger to me means loss of control, and I'm not the kind of person who loses control. It is counter-productive and inappropriate, and doesn't gain anything of value.

When I feel stress building, instead of getting angry or impatient, I step back, take a deep breath and begin to focus on the positives. The results are quite dramatic, my whole demeanor changes very rapidly,

I have the power to choose my attitude and control my own thoughts, so I choose to stay in control.

What are some of the things that bother you?

I enjoy my work, and believe in giving value to my employer. Dealing with clock watchers, and the ones who regularly get sick on Mondays and Friday's concerns me, but it's not something that gets me angry or anything like that.

Managing Adversity...

How do you react to criticism?

Criticism is vital to my continued growth, and I welcome constructive criticism that helps me operate better or produce better results. However, it is important for me to understand where my critic is coming from so that I know how to apply the feedback.

I look for the good in what the other person is saying. I don't read between the lines, nor add meaning or implications where none were intended. When the other person has finished, I ask any questions that are needed, and seek recommendations or ideas that will readily improve the situation.

I would express regret over the situation then thank the person for raising the issue. If I intend to act on what I've heard, I let the other person know.

How do you handle personal criticism?

As long as the criticism is fair and constructive, I listen to it and remain gracious. I thank them for their candid feedback, and modify my future behaviour accordingly.

Do you work well under pressure?

Absolutely. How you react to pressure depends very much on how you perceive it. Because pressure is the result of a new challenge, I perceive pressure as an opportunity to develop and grow. The more challenges I experience, the better my skills become, and the less I feel the pressure of subsequent challenges. So, because I am committed to developing myself, I welcome the challenges of pressure.

How would I know you were under pressure?

I disguise my pressure well, therefore, you wouldn't know if I were under pressure.

How do you approach difficult situations?

I approach difficult situations in a calm and objective way and am polite yet resolute when handling a difficult customer.

Before making a judgement, I stand back, observe and try to establish the facts by asking questions and listening, I then act professionally and try to seek acceptable outcomes for all those involved.

If a solution cannot be found, I try to aim for a win-win situation, so that there are no feelings of loss on either side.

How have you benefited/learned from your mistakes?

I have learned a lot from mistakes, either my own or those of others. Whenever I make a mistake, I acknowledge the error, and use it as a lesson to keep me from making the same mistake again. That way I never repeat mistakes, and always anticipate potential problems.

How would you deal with a supervisor who is unfair or difficult to work with?

If the behaviour is a regular pattern, and not a chance occurrence or the result of stress, I would make an appointment to see the supervisor.

During our appointment, I would diplomatically explain that I feel uncomfortable in our professional relationship, that I feel he or she is not treating me as a professional. I would then ask for his or her input.

There are many times when the person may or may not know that his/her behaviour is causing a problem for you, and talking to him or her can clear up what turns out to be a simple misunderstanding.

How do you criticise others?

I don't really criticise, because I don't feel it is a constructive way to approach others, but I do try to offer constructive feedback.

When I have an opinion to express, I gather my thoughts, formulate my ideas, and then present them to the other person privately.

I ensure the conversation focuses on any business discrepancies, and does not get personal or spiral into blame. I also ensure that all feedback I give is as positive as possible so that the person on the receiving end thinks that any bad messages are balanced by their positive attributes, and I always finish the conversation on a positive note.

Can you take brief and direct instructions without feeling upset?

Yes, I take instructions well, and I recognise that it comes in two varieties depending on the circumstances. There are carefully explained instructions, then there are those times when, as a result of deadlines and other pressures, the instruction might be brief and to the point. While I have seen some people get upset with that, personally I've always understood that there are probably other considerations I am not aware of. So I listen very carefully to directions, and always keep my superior informed of my actions.

What are some of the things you find difficult to do?

I find it difficult to do nothing, I have to be doing something.

Work Ethics...

What do you feel is a satisfactory attendance record?

I believe it is every employee's responsibility to show up, on time, every workday. Days lost through sickness are unproductive and expensive and should only be taken when absolutely necessary. I think you owe it to your colleagues as well as your manager to be punctual.

What is your attendance record like?

I'm proud to say that my attendance record has always been very good. I'm in excellent health, I don't have any allergies, and I rebound quickly. I have never had to cancel an appointment due to sickness and in the whole time I was working at Aspire Hair & Beauty, I only took three days off for an extremely heavy cold. I am usually pretty resilient, and more often than not, I manage to arrange any medical appointments around my work.

Do you arrive at work on time?

Yes, I am usually the first to arrive in the morning, and I dislike being late for anything. If I have a problem being on time due to traffic, car trouble, etc, I always call ahead to explain the situation.

What motivates you to work hard?

I have always been self motivated. I like that winning feeling when I do a good job. The sense of achievement motivates me to make even bigger efforts.

I also like being surrounded by capable and hard working colleagues. The energy and creativity people can activate in each other is amazing.

Other great motivators include: Daily challenges, personal growth, accepting responsibility, encouragement to use creativity and initiative, and finally, respect for a job well done.

Does money motivate you to work hard?

Although I consider remuneration an important motivational factor, it is a secondary importance. The job itself, its tasks, the work environment and the opportunity to are to me the most significant aspects of a job.

What do you do when you find it difficult to do your best work?

I rarely find it difficult to do my best work, I am always motivated to give my best efforts, and there are always opportunities to contribute when you stay alert.

When, for various reasons, it becomes difficult to do my best work, I find myself driving to produce, to maintain my record of success.

People
Skills...

How do you get along with different kinds of people?

I like contact with colleagues and clients, and would generally describe myself as a very sociable person. I have very good interpersonal skills, and I pride myself on being able to build rapport quickly with new people.

To me, establishing rapport seems to be a natural tendency. In fact, at Aspire Hair & Beauty, I was often asked to carry out the shampoo because the manager knew I would make the clients feel welcome and important.

Communication Competence...

How confident are you about addressing a group?

I used to be nervous about speaking in front of a group, yet I found that preparation, practice and knowing my subject helped me overcome this, I now have no problem addressing a grou

Rate your communication skills on a scale of 1 to 10 with 10 representing excellent communication skills.

I would rate myself as an 8. I always give my best, but in doing so I increase my skills. I, therefore, always see room for improvement.

Teamwork...

Are you a good team player?

Absolutely. I am self motivated, I respect other people's opinions, I communicate well with my colleagues, and I can be relied on to pull with the team.

Do you prefer to work alone or as part of a team?

Whether I prefer to work as part of a team or alone depend on the best way to complete the job. Either way, I am equally happy, and I am equally efficient in both.

I do, however, prefer team spirit. In a team, people learn from each other and tend to achieve results faster, more efficiently and with greater satisfaction.

What do you enjoy most about working as part of a team?

There's nothing like being part of a great team where you can learn from the other members, bounce ideas off one another, and share achievements and rewards. There is a unique feeling of camaraderie that can never be experienced from working alone.

What do you least enjoy about working as part of a team?

People not pulling their weight, is the least enjoyable aspect of working in a team, however, I've noticed that such people simply lack enthusiasm or confidence, and that energetic and cheerful co-workers can often change that.

What do you find most challenging about being part of a team?

The most challenging aspect is inspiring and motivating other team members. Each has different needs and is motivated by different things.

In a team situation, do you take on a leader or follower role?

I am both a leader and follower. If a situation comes up and someone has to take charge, and I feel I can, then I will. But if someone else has already taken charge and is solving it, I will follow. I am whatever I need to be.

Do you try hard to get colleagues to like you?

It is in my nature to try to get on with everyone I work with, and I input a lot of effort into building trustworthy business relationships. If a colleague doesn't like me, I will see if there is anything I can do to change their perspective, but if I cannot, I will be respectful and professional towards them so that we can at least continue to have a professional working relationship, where personal feelings do not interfere with the work.

How would you define teamwork?

I define teamwork as a group of people who work cooperatively with one another to achieve a common goal. There is a coordinated effort between the members, and each individual contributes their unique skills, puts their preferences aside and pulls their own weight to reach a positive conclusion.

What is your definition of a good employee?

A good employee assumes responsibility, always works to the best of their abilities, and is interested in improving. They communicate well and appropriately, feel and show team spirit, appreciate differences and show respect for others. They are reliable, trustworthy and can appreciate criticism, not just tolerate or accept it but benefit from it too.

What do you think enables a team to work well together?

Essentially teams work well together when there is strong team commitment, open communication and good leadershi They have respect for each other and the organisation they are part of, feelings are expressed freely, and conflict is faced up and worked through.

What do you think prevents a team working well together?

Teams may break down because lack of communication or poor leadership, or the root cause might be something relatively trivial like, clash of personalities, lack of motivation, and trust.

Describe your ideal work grou

My ideal work group would be one which has an infusion of character among the participants, where the members are able to inspire and motivate each other, while retaining mutual trust and respect.

There is open communication and good leadership, and everyone is motivated to achieve a common aim. Decisions are made by consensus, feelings are expressed freely, and conflict is faced up and worked through.

How well do you lead people?

I try to lead by example and I've experienced good results from the leadership side of my work. I'm pleased that those I initially trained and supervised eventually moved on to positions of greater responsibilities.

Customer Service...

What do you find most challenging about providing customer service?

Providing customer service in general is a challenge. People are unpredictable by nature, so you have to expect the unexpected, and be prepared to go beyond the call of duty.

I enjoy the challenges of providing customer care. I think it's something I'm good at.

What do you most enjoy about providing customer care?

The most enjoyable aspect I would have to say is that because I genuinely care about my client's satisfaction, it rewards me personally when I know that they are happy with the job I did, which in turn drives me to do better.

What do you least enjoy about providing customer care?

Providing good customer care can be a challenge, and some people may view that negatively, but I view each challenge as an opportunity to develop and grow. So, because I am committed to developing myself, I welcome, and even enjoy, the challenges of providing customer care. It is something I have become very adept to.

How would you define good customer service?

Good customer service is about constantly and consistently meeting customer's expectations by providing a friendly, efficient and reliable service throughout the life of the service and/or product.

Excellent customer service is about exceeding customer's expectations by going beyond the call of duty. No two customers are the same, and so they deserve to receive a service that is tailored to their individual needs. I believe this is where a service moves beyond being just a satisfactory one, and becomes an excellent one.

What do you think constitutes poor customer service?

Poor customer service is when customer's expectations are met by rude, ignorant and unknowledgeable staff who provides a poor quality product and/or service, while showing disrespect and a lack of courtesy toward the customer,

Do you think the customer is always right?

Absolutely not. Whilst every customer is important, those who exhibit abusive behaviour, or do anything to compromise safety are straying beyond the boundary.

When have you witnessed good customer service?

I went to a local Harverster restaurant for a luncheon. It was only 2pm on a Wednesday afternoon, but much to my surprise, they were exceptionally busy, and only had three waiting staff on duty.

Despite the overwhelming rush, Claire, the waitress was polite and helpful. The staff showed great teamwork, and, as a result, managed to deliver outstanding service.

When have you witnessed poor customer service?

I needed a particular material for a dress I was making. In most stores the salesperson would give me a quick 'no' before I finished explaining what I was looking for.

I hadn't really noticed until I experienced the opposite service in another smaller fabric store.

Analytical
Skills...

Decision Making...

How do you go about making important decisions?

Before I act, I think. I evaluate my options and examine them objectively, weighing up possible outcomes, pros and cons, etc. I then rely on past experiences, company policies, intuition and common sense to guide me to a decision.

I present my planned solution to those who will be affected by it, such as colleagues, as well as those who will be called upon to explain my decision, my superiors. I then implement appropriate input and suggestions where necessary.

What decisions do you dislike making?

The kinds of decisions I dislike making, are the ones which result in customer dissatisfaction, such as having to cancel or postpone an appointment, for example. When the client is dissatisfied, I feel dissatisfied.

I accept that these kinds of decisions cannot always be avoided, and so I deal with them efficiently as they arise, but I try to arrive at a solution that produces the best results for the company, while minimising the effects on the customer.

What decisions do you find most difficult?

It's not that I have difficulties making decisions, some just require more consideration than others.

Problem Solving...

In your current/past position, what problems did you come across that came as a surprise to you?

By planning ahead, I can anticipate any potential problems and be prepared to deal with them, rather than be surprised by them.

However, because life is unpredictable by its very nature, there will always be some problems that arise and cannot be prepared for. When these arise, I take appropriate action as necessary.

Shortly after I began freelancing, there was a three day postal strike, and my supplies were seriously delayed. Without the supplies, I couldn't book any appointments. While a postal strike was an obvious potential risk that I had considered, it took me by surprise because I didn't expect it to become a problem so soon in my freelance career. Luckily, I was able to resolve the problem with no serious or long term consequences.

How do you prepare yourself for potential problems?

I prepare for potential problems by analysing past problems.

By planning ahead, I can anticipate any potential problems and be prepared to deal with them. I keep comparing my current situation against my plan, and take necessary action to correct any deviation. This helps me expect and prepare for problems, rather than be surprised by them.

Naturally, because life is unpredictable by nature, there will always be some unexpected problems that arise and cannot be prepared for. When these arise, I take appropriate action as necessary.

I stand back and examine the problem. I make a list of possible solutions, weighing both the consequences and cost of each solution to determine the best course of action. I then present my planned solution to those who will be affected by it, and seek advice and/or approval.

What do you do when you have trouble solving a problem?

One thing I don't do is ignore it and hope it will go away. I stand back and examine the problem. I make a list of possible solutions, weighing both the consequences and cost of each solution to determine the best course of action. I then present my planned solution to those who will be affected by it, and seek advice and/or approval.

Miscellaneous...

What do you do to relax after a hard day?

After a hard day, I like to make a break from the environment and unwind. If time permits, I either go for a swim, a sauna or perform my yoga and relaxation routines. Otherwise, I like to cook a nice meal, followed by a relaxing soak in a nice warm bath.

What is your energy level like?

My energy levels are on top form. To keep them that way I routinely involve myself in cardiovascular exercise. If you have too much energy, cardiovascular exercise uses some of it u If I have too little, it stimulates the body's systems and finds you some.

What do your family think about you applying for this position?

My family understand the decision I have made. They support me 100%.

Has anyone in the business world ever been an inspiration to you?

Yes, several people. During my working life, I have been fortunate to have worked with some very skilled people who were exceptionally good at certain aspects of their role, and who have influenced me.

Through observation and discussion, I have identified what made them good at what they do, and have tried to follow their examples. I think I've learned an even greater amount from these individuals than from text books I've read, and the courses I've taken?

Who was the most influential person in your life?

I have been most influenced by my manager at Aspire Hair & Beauty. From the time I began working at the salon, she took a sincere interest in my work, and under her guidance, I grew personally and professionally.

She taught me many necessary skills and work methods, and provided constant motivation and encouragement for my efforts. We always felt mutual trust and respect for one another, and I consider myself very fortunate to have had her by my side early in my career, as a supervisor, teacher and remarkable person.

What question could I ask you that would really intimidate you?

I can't think of any question that would intimidate me. This is probably the most intimidating question.

How would you rate me as a recruiter?

First, I'd give you high marks for your people skills. You helped me feel at ease right away, which made it easier for me to answer the questions. I'd also rate you highly on the creativity of the questions, and their thoroughness. By probing me as carefully as you have, you've given me a better opportunity to secure this position. You've given me a complete picture of what to expect at Aspire Airlines, and it confirms my belief that this is where I want to work.

Do you feel appearance is important?

Yes, appearance is very important in terms of being neat, clean and tidy. Your appearance contributes to whether people will have the confidence in you, and the ability to inspire confidence is a great asset.

What don't you like to do?

I don't particularly enjoy doing paperwork, because it seems to slow down the action. However, I realise the importance of documentation, so I cooperatively fill out any forms, but I'm always looking for efficiencies in that area that will get me out in front of the customer where I belong.

When there's something disagreeable to be done, I try to get it out of the way first.

Are you able to work alone without direct supervision?

Absolutely. Owing to the nature of my occupation, and the kind of tasks that I carry out in my job, I regularly work independently. I am a self starter and don't need constant reassurance.

How do you feel about company rules and policies?

I consider company rules, policies and procedures necessary for the efficient running of any business. They ensure that fairness, consistency and safety measures are applied across the board, and that the right work environment is created and maintained. They help people make decisions, and give them a sense of direction. My policy is always to observe the rules, and make sure my colleagues observe them as well.

Have you ever felt constraints and had to go against policies to reach your goal?

We all feel the constraints of some policies and procedures from time to time. However, to achieve uniformity and consistency, and to ensure that relevant standards and regulations are followed, it is necessary to have those policies and procedures in place. It is always possible to cut corners and achieve the required results sooner or with less effort, but I have never taken the path of least resistance.

To get the job done people sometimes have to bend the truth. Have you ever done the same thing?

I have never bent the truth, and have always abided by company policies. I believe this is the key to being a professional and successful employee.

Have you ever worked for a superior who was younger, or less experienced than yourself?

I haven't worked for such a superior. My former superiors were very experienced professionals who were older than myself, from whom I've learned a lot.

In either case, I am comfortable working with any age grou I don't consider age to be an important factor, what matters is a person's credibility, professionalism and competency.

Do you get bored doing the same work over and over again?

No. Work is not necessarily entertaining, it is something that must be routinely and successfully accomplished, time after time. That's why it is called work, and why I am being paid to do it. Sometimes you just have to set your preferences aside, and focus on what needs to be done, even if it isn't something new and exciting.

Wrap
It Up...

How do you feel about the six-month probationary period?

I can see no problem with a probationary period. I am a fast learner, and it shouldn't take me long to prove myself.

Do you have any reservations about working here?

I see this position as a fine opportunity, and the airline as one I would be proud to be an employee of. I don't have any reservations at this point.

Can we take it then that you do still wish us to consider you for this post?

Absolutely! Having had this chance to meet you and learn more about your operation and what the post will entail, I am even keener than before. I am convinced that this is the opportunity I am seeking, and I know I can make a positive contribution.

If one of our competitors offered you a job now, would you take it?

Because I am set on making cabin crew my future career, if I did not get this job with Aspire, then I would have to consider other airlines. However, Aspire Airlines are at the very top of my list.

Would you take this job if we offered it to you?

Yes, definitely. I was keen as soon as I saw the job opening on the web site. More than that though, actually meeting potential colleagues and finding out more about your current activities has clarified still further what an exciting challenge it would be to work here.

When are you available to start work if offered the position?

I have the energy and enthusiasm to start straight away. All I need is a week's notice and I'm ready.

How would you respond if we told you that you have been unsuccessful on this occasion?

Naturally, it will be a disappointment if I do not secure this job with Aspire because it is something I really want, I feel ready for it, and I have had plenty of experience to contribute. However, I am not one to give up quickly. I will think about where I went wrong and how I could have done better, and I would then take steps towards strengthening my candidacy.

Have you stretched the truth today to gain a favourable outcome?

No, I haven't tried to be someone I am not, because I wouldn't want to get the job that way. To win that way would be such a short term gain because eventually I would be found out.

Are you willing to start as a trainee?

Yes, definitely. This is a new area for me, and I believe in getting a good foundation in the basics before progressing. An entry level position will enable me to learn the position inside out, and will give me the opportunity to grow when I prove myself. I also have a great deal of knowledge and work experience, which I'm sure will contribute to my rapid progress through training.

What would you say if I said your skills and experience were below the requirements of this job?

I would ask what particular aspects of my skills and experience you felt were lacking and address each one of those areas with examples of where my skills and experiences do match your requirements. I would expect that after this discussion you would be left in no doubt about my ability to do this job.

Can we contact your previous employers for references/What would they say?

Yes, absolutely. I'm confident that all my references will be favourable and will confirm what we've discussed here today.

Hypothetical
Questions...

People Management (234)

Managing Adversity (237)

Hypothetical questions present candidates with difficult real-life situations, where almost any answer can be challenged.

A good way to approach these questions is to consider the feelings of all involved, and think about the implications for your colleagues and the airline.

Prove to your recruiters that you would be proactive and do your best to resolve the situation using your own initiative, whilst remembering that you could ask for the help of the more experienced crew if necessary.

If you have followed these guidelines, and are still challenged, the recruiter may be testing your ability to manage conflict, or stress. Bear in mind that if you are not cabin crew yet, you cannot really be expected to know the best reply so do not be tricked into entering into an argument with the recruiter.

In either case, it is important to remain calm, focused, and to demonstrate that although you appreciate there are many aspects to each situation, you would always be trying to find acceptable solutions.

If you really can't think of a solution, you can simply say, "That is a new area for me, so I am afraid I can't really answer that, but I enjoy acquiring new knowledge, and I do learn quickly."

People Management...

You are in flight at 30,000 feet. How would you handle a passenger if he became irate about his lost baggage?

At 30,000 feet, there is not a lot you can do about the baggage, so the problem at hand is reassuring the passenger and avoiding further disruption.

First, I would try to manoeuvre the passenger somewhere more private where they can quietly tell me about the situation, I would then apologise for the mishandling, and offer to assist on the ground by escorting him to the proper people who can hel

What would you do if the seat belt signs are on because of turbulence, but a passenger gets up to go to the toilet?

In non fatal accidents, turbulence is the biggest cause of injuries to both passengers and crew, therefore, I would advise the passenger to wait until the seatbelt signs are turned off.

If the passenger really cannot wait, I will follow the corporate policy for dealing with such a situation.

How would you handle a passenger who is intoxicated?

I would not provide any more alcoholic drinks. I would also encourage food, and offer a cup of tea or coffee. If the situation does not improve, or worsens beyond my control, I would inform my senior and seek assistance from the other crew members.

What would you do if a commercially important passenger complained about a crying child?

I would apologise to the passenger and offer my assistance to the guardian of the crying child.

How would you deal with a passenger who is scared of flying?

I would try to comfort the passenger by talking them through the flight, and reassuring them of any strange noises they may hear.

Being aware of what to expect, and just realising that a plane's wings are supposed to flex and move around gently in flight, can help relieve anxiety. Similarly, the collection of bumps and bangs that always accompany a flight can be made less fearsome if they are expected.

I would tell them where I can be found, and show them the call bell. I would then check on them periodically throughout the flight.

How would you handle a colleague who comes to you in tears?

I would take them aside, and try to determine the cause of their upset. If it were something that I could assist with, I would offer them my time. If it were a personal problem, I would listen, and offer my empathy and support.

How would you deal with a passenger who is not, right but believes he is right?

I would explain the company's rules and policies to the passenger in a calm, professional and positive manner. Hopefully, this should clarify any misconceptions that the passenger may have.

What would you do if a co-worker were not pulling their weight?

I've noticed that such people simply lack enthusiasm, and even confidence, and that energetic and cheerful co workers can often change that. So when I feel others are not pulling their weight, I first try to overcome it with a positive attitude that I hope will catch on. If this does nothing, I will try to reason with and challenge the person. Failing that, I will need to consider seeking advice from a senior member of staff.

How would you handle a colleague who is being rude or racist?

I would act immediately to put a stop to any racist or rude behaviour by making it clear to the person that their behaviour is not acceptable. If he or she continues, I would then report it to proper authority.

If you spotted a colleague doing something unethical or illegal, what would you do?

I would act immediately to put a stop to any unethical or illegal activity. I would try to document the details of the incident and try to collect any physical evidence. Then I would report it to my senior.

What would you do if you felt your superior was dishonest, incompetent or had a personal problem?

That would depend on the seriousness of the problem and whether or not it was affecting his ability to do his job.

Obviously in the case of dishonesty or incompetence, action would be required. A personal problem might, or might not affect others in the workplace, and I would need to make a judgement on the individual case.

Managing
Adversity...

How are you going to cope if a passenger vents his frustrations on you?

Wearing the airline's uniform, it is expected that people will view you as a representative of the airline, and a target to vent their frustrations upon.

I simply see it as part of the work. I will not take it personally, I will remain calm, be professional and continue to offer the best service I can.

What would you do if you suspect that a passenger is suspicious or a high risk to passengers?

I would report to the senior any abnormal behaviour indicating a suspicious passenger.

What would you do and how would you react in a hijacking?

I would remain calm, and follow the emergency guidelines and procedures.

How would you act in an emergency?

I treat a crisis like a crisis. I move quickly, confidently, and authoritatively in those situations where decisive action is required.

How would you act in an emergency such as a crash landing?

As soon as I get the warning that something is going to happen, I would get a plan together in my mind. I would stay calm and in control and follow the emergency guidelines and procedures.

What would you do if you received a telephone call telling you that a family member had been taken ill?

I would ring home, at the earliest convenience, to get updates. If it was something extremely serious, then I would hope that my employer would understand the need for me to take time off work at the earliest convenience. If, on the other hand, the situation was not so serious, I would continue with my work as necessary.

What three items would you choose to have if trapped on a desert island?

The three items I would have to have would be a medical kit containing various items such as medicines, water purification tablets, surgical blades, plasters and cotton wool, etc. Second, I would have my survival kit containing essential items such as a compass, a striker and flint, torch, waterproof matches, a magnifying glass, and fish hooks and line, etc. Third, a survival pouch containing fuel tablets, flexible saw, signal flares, a radio transmitter, brew kit and food.

If you were trapped on a desert island, what book would you want?

I would have to have my pocket sized 'Collins Gem, SAS survival guide'. The guide is packed full of practical advice on survival in the wild, from how to attract attention to yourself so that rescuers may find you, to making your way across unknown territory back to civilisation if there is no hope of rescue, and everything in between.

If you were going to Mars, what three items would you take?

First, I would take a trained astronaut. Second, sufficient food for the journey. Finally, enough fuel for the return tri

Questions
For the Recruiter...

This section of the interview is a real chance for you to shine and set yourself apart from all the other candidates. Therefore, it is a good idea to prepare one or two intelligent questions in advance.

The questions you ask, and how you ask them, say a lot about you, your motives, your depth of knowledge about the airline and the position itself.

Guidelines

Your questions should follow these guidelines:

- Don't ask questions that could be easily answered through your own research.
- Ask questions which demonstrate a genuine interest in and knowledge of the airline and the position.
- Your questions should also demonstrate that you know just that little bit more than is required.

Question About Suitability

Asking recruiters to raise their concerns about your suitability will provide you with an opportunity to follow up and reassure the recruiter.

- Do you have any reservations about my ability to do this job?
- What do you foresee as possible obstacles or problems I might have?
- Is there anything else I need to do to maximise my chances of getting this job?
- How does my background compare with others you have interviewed?
- Is there anything else you'd like to know?
- What do you think are my strongest assets and possible weaknesses?
- Do you have any concerns that I need to clear up in order to be the top candidate?

Questions About the Recruiter

Asking recruiters about their views and experience in the job or working with the airline will demonstrate your genuine interest and motives.

- How did you find the transition in relocating to ___?
- Why did you choose to work at ___ airlines?
- What is it about this airline that keeps you working here?
- It sounds as if you really enjoy working here, what have you enjoyed most about working for ___ airlines?

General Questions

- How would you describe the company culture?
- I feel my background and experience are a good fit for this position, and I am very interested. What is the next step?
- Yes, when do I start?

No Questions

-
- I did have plenty of questions, but we've covered them all during our discussions. I was particularly interested in __, but we've dealt with that thoroughly.
- I had many questions, but you've answered them all you have been so helpful. I'm even more excited about this opportunity than when I applied.
-

Questions to Avoid

You should avoid asking questions such as those following as they will make you appear selfishly motivated.

- How many day's holiday allowances will I receive?
- What is the salary?
- When will I receive a pay increase?
- How many free flights will my family receive?
- Can I request flights to ___?

The Closing Stage

Part 10

Making a Successful Close

Gather your belongings, and ensure you have a tight grip on them.

Stand up, straighten your clothes, and shake hands with your recruiter(s). When shaking hands, simply say "Thank you very much for providing time from your busy schedule to meet with me today. I look forward to hearing from you." Smile and make your way to the door.

Stop at the door, turn, smile, and ten exit the room, closing the door quietly behind you.

Closing Mistakes to Avoid

Regardless of what has happened, and regardless of how you are feeling, it is important that you leave the interview room in a positive frame of mind, as if it were a complete success

Oftentimes, we feel uncertain, and even overly critical, about our performance, but may have made a better impression that we realise. Leaving the room dejected will not leave the recruiters with a positive impression about your ability to manage adversity, and may even negatively influence the recruiter's decision.

Likewise, making a dash for the door will make you appear unconfident, and even disinterested. Plus, you may trip over yourself, or fumble over your belongings, which is certainly not a good look.

Post
Interview

Part 11

What Happens Next?

Following the final interview, airlines aim to respond with an outcome within two to eight weeks. Those who have been unsuccessful will usually receive a computer generated letter advising them of the unfortunate outcome.

If, on the other hand, you are one of the fortunate few who have been successful, you will receive an email, phone call and/or letter from the recruitment department.

At this stage, you will be advised of the various pre-joining clearance requirements. These may include:

- A pre-employment medical test
- Reference checks
- Joining forms

Once the required steps of the process have been completed, the airline will make the necessary arrangements to deliver the employment contract and relevant documentation. You will also be given final clearance to resign from your current employer and, subsequently, a copy of your accepted resignation may be requested.

Note that in some cases, employment contracts will be dispatched to candidates prior to the clearances being given, however, the contract terms clearly state that the validity of the employment contract is subject to obtaining these pre-joining clearances. If you receive the contract prior to clearance being given, do not resign from your current employment until you are formally advised to do so by the recruitment team.

Follow-up Letters

Following your interview, it is a good idea to follow up with a letter or email expressing appreciation and thanks for the interview.

It is a great opportunity to make a further positive impression, plus, it will make you stand out if none of your competitor's bother.

The purpose of this letter is to:

- Show appreciation for the employer's interest in you.
- Reiterate your interest in the position, and in the airline.
- Review or remind the employer about your qualifications for the position.
- Demonstrate that you have good manners.
- Follow up with any information the employer may have asked you to provide after the interview.
- Address unresolved points.

Guidelines

When you write your thank you letter, use these guidelines:

Format
Emails are convenient to send, which also means that they are perceived as being far less personal. Traditional hard copy letters are much more formal, and the recruiter is more likely to read it. So, unless you have been requested otherwise, you should opt for the latter.

Email is appropriate if your primary means of communication with the recruitment team has been through online channels, or if the recruiter has expressed a preference for email communication.

Typed or Handwritten
Handwritten letters are more personal, however, if your penmanship is lacking, you should consider a typed format, or have someone write the final draft for you.

Use quality plain white or ivory paper
Fancy papers can appear chea Instead of using colour paper, or uneccessary, over the top glossy and parchment papers, stick to using a high quality white or ivory paper.

Send your letter within 24 hours
You should write your letter right away while the experience is still fresh in your memory.

Hard copies should be sent within 24 hours of your interview. Emails can be sent that same evening, so that it is in the recruiter's inbox the next morning.

Personalize it
If you met with more than one recruiter, consider extending the courtesy by sending them all thank you letters.

Thank the Interviewer
Everyone likes to feel that his or her time is respected, so the first thing you should do is thank the recruiter for taking the time to meet with you.

Express your enthusiasm
Be sure that the tone of the letter conveys your interest and enthusiasm for both the job, and the airline. You could also reiterate your suitability. Don't overdo it though as you may appear desperate.

Address unresolved points
If necessary, you could use the opportunity to address any issues or questions that came up during the interview that you feel you did not fully answer.

Don't oversell
You don't want to oversell yourself on the thank you letter, so keep the letter clean, focused and to the point.

Making a successful close
Close out the thank you letter by offering to provide additional information if they have any questions, and tell them that you're looking forward to hearing back from them on a decision.

Proofread
Your letter is going to be read by the recruiter, and it may be the final impression you leave with that person before they make a hiring decision.

Make sure you convey a professional image by being certain that it reads well, and is free from spelling mistakes and grammatical errors. If possible, have a trusted friend proofread it before you send it out.

Figure 16: Sample Follow-up Letter

16 Any Road • AnyWhere
Any Town • AN8 9SE
United Kingdom
(+44) 04587 875848 • janedoe@anymail.com

FAO: Mr. J Doe
Human Resources Manager
Aspire Airline   25th July 2007
Cabin Crew Recruitment
O. BOX 29
London
United Kingdom

Dear Mr. Doe

Thank you very much for providing time from your busy schedule to talk with me about the cabin crew position at Aspire Airlines. I truly appreciate your time and consideration in interviewing me.

I felt a wonderful rapport, not only with you, but with all the team members I met with. I am further convinced that I will compliment your team and make a positive contribution to the airline's ongoing success.

As you requested, I have enclosed a list of references whom you may contact to further confirm my prior work accomplishments.

I am very interested in working for you and look forward to hearing from you once the final decisions are made. Please feel free to contact me if you need any further information.

Sincerely,

Jane Doe
Encl

Pre-Employment Medical Examination

You will be required to undergo a pre-employment medical examination before officially being offered a contract of employment.

Depending on the airline, the examination may be conducted in your home country at your own expense, at the airline's designated medical centre at the ailrine's expense, or both.

The examination will generally consist of:

- HIV/Aids Test
- Haemoglobin
- Chest x-ray
- Pap or Cervical Smear Test
- Audiogram
- Ophthalmic Report
- Certificate of Dental Health and Dental x-rays

You will also be required to be completely up to date on your vaccinations, including the following:

- Polio
- Diphtheria
- Tetanus
- Typhoid
- Hepatitis A&B,
- Rubella (females only)
- Tuberculin Skin Test
- BCG Vaccination

See the following page for an example of a medical examination requirement form.

Figure 17: Sample Pre-Employment Medical Examination Guidelines

ASPIRE AIRLINES
PRE-EMPLOYMENT MEDICAL EXAMINATION

1.0   Introduction to the Medical

1.1   The primary aim of the medical is to ensure that the applicant does not suffer from any disease or disability that could suddenly render him/her unable to perform his/her assigned duties safely.

1.2   The medical comprises of three main areas:

- Physical and Mental Requirements
- Eye Sight Check
- Hearing Check

2.0   Physical and Mental Requirements

2.1 following   The applicant should have no established medical history or diagnosis of any of the ailments:

- Psychiatric or psychological problems including depression
- Alcoholism
- Any personality disorder, particularly if severe enough to have resulted in self injury
- A mental abnormality, or neurosis of a significant degree
- Drug dependence (The applicant will be drug screened as a pre-employment requirement. Candidates should avoid taking any sleeping tablets or cold remedies in the week prior to this.)

2.2   The applicant shall have no established medical history or clinical diagnosis of any of the following:

- A progressive or non-progressive disease of the nervous system, the effects of which, are likely to interfere with the safe exercise of the applicants duties
- Epilepsy
- Any disturbance of consciousness without satisfactory medical explanation of cause
- Cases of head injury with sequelae that are likely to interfere with the safe exercise of the applicants duties

2.3   The applicant shall not possess any abnormality of the heart, congenital or acquired, which is likely to interfere with the safe exercise of the applicant's duties. A history of proven myocardial infarction shall be disqualifying. Such commonly occurring conditions as respiratory arrhythmia (irregular rhythm of the heart), occasional extra systoles (or heart beats) which disappear on exercise, increase in pulse rate from excitement or exercise, or a slow pulse not associated with heart conduction disorders may be regarded as being within "normal" limits.

2.4   The Systolic and Diastolic blood pressures shall be within normal limits.

2.5   There shall be no significant functional or structure abnormality of the circulatory system.

2.6   There shall be no acute disability of the lungs or any active disease of the structure of the lungs, chest or lung cavities. Radiography will form a part of the initial chest examination.

2.7   Cases of asthma or breathing difficulties, including shortness of breath, or wheezing shall be assessed as unfit if the condition is causing symptoms. A history of asthma as a child is acceptable if the condition is in complete remission without the need for preventative medications.

2.8   Cases of active pulmonary tuberculosis shall be assessed as unfit. Cases of quiescent or healed lesions may be assessed as fit.

2.9   Cases of disabling disease with impairment of function of the gastrointestinal tract or its adnexa shall be assessed as unfit.

2.10   The applicant shall be required to be completely free from those hernias or ruptures that might give rise to incapacitating symptoms. Any results of disease or surgical intervention on any part of the digestive tract or its adnexa, liable to cause incapacity in flight or reduce ability to work as required by the airline, in particular any obstructions due to stricture or compression shall be assessed as unfit.

2.11   Cases of metabolic, nutritional or endocrine disorders (e.g. diabetes) likely to interfere with the safe exercise of the applicant's licence and rating privileges shall be assessed as unfit.

2.12   Cases of significant localised and generalised enlargement of the lymphatic glands and diseases of the blood shall be assessed as unfit, except in cases where accredited medical conclusion indicates that the condition indicates that the condition is not likely to affect the safe exercise of the applicant's duties.

3.0   Eye Sight Check

3.1   The following are the requirements for eye sight of Cabin Crew

- Good Binocular Vision
- Distant Visual Acuity, with correction by contact lenses (if necessary), to 6/9 (20/30) or better
- Near Vision Acuity, with correction by contact lenses (if necessary), to read N5 at 30-50cm and N14 at 100cm
- Currently, spectacles cannot be worn and so only contact lenses are acceptable for visual correction. These lenses should be suitable for long-term wear in the dry aircraft environment. Soft permeable lenses are preferable and those candidates who require hard lenses (e.g. keratoconus) are not suitable.

4.0   Hearing Check

4.1   The applicant, tested on a pure-tone audiometer at the first issue of silence, shall not have a hearing loss, in either ear separately, of more than 35dB at any of the frequencies 500, 1,000 or 2,000 Hz, or more than 50dB at 3,000 Hz. However an applicant with a hearing loss greater than the above may be declared fit provided that:

- The applicant has a hearing performance in each ear separately equivalent to that of a normal person, against a background noise that will stimulate the masking properties of flight deck noise upon speech and beacon signals; and
- The applicant has the ability to hear an average conversation voice in a quiet room using both ears, at a distance of 2 meters (6 feet) from the examiner, with the back turned to the examiner

Training

Successful candidates will be required to attend an intensive training program. Dependent on the airline's requirements, training usually lasts between four to eight weeks, and covers both the practical and theoretical aspects of the cabin service.

While intensive, the training is delivered in a fun and informative way through lots of practical exercises. You can expect non-stop action as you will be shooting down inflatable slides during evacuation simulations, fighting fires in mock cabins and performing life saving CPR on training dummies.

To graduate from cabin crew program, you will need to pass regular assessments on all subjects studied on the course. Each module has stringent pass marks, and so you will need to allow plenty of time for revision outside the classroom.

In the event of exam failure, you are usually permitted one re-sit. Alternatively, you will be given the opportunity to join another training group, which is a week or two behind. A subsequent failure of an exam would result in withdrawal from the course, hence a high standard of performance and dedication is required.

The first six months of flying duties are probationary, and are seen as a continuation of this initial training,. During this period, you will receive further on-board training and assessments. Following probation, you can expect yearly assessments.

The Other Side of the Desk

Part 12

Recruiters will usually refer to a competency rating scale when determining your suitability for the position.

The scale works on a points based system, and your answers will reflect the score you receive for each required competency.

The forms and scales will vary from airline to airline, thus, the sample forms on the following pages have been included for illustration purposes only.

Competency Rating Forms

Figure 18: Sample Competency Rating Form

Competency	Definition	Rating
Action Oriented	Consistently maintains high levels of activity or productivity.	
Adaptability	Adapts well to change.	
Applied Learning	Introduces newly gained knowledge and skills on the job.	
Building Trust	Is seen as direct and truthful, keeps confidences, promises, and commitments.	
Collaboration	Builds constructive working relationships with clients and customers. Behaves professionally and supportively when working with individuals from a variety of ethnic, social and educational backgrounds.	
Communication	Demonstrates good written, oral, and listening skills	
Conflict Management	Uses appropriate interpersonal styles and techniques to reduce tension and/or conflict between two or more people.	
Continuous Learning and Professional Development	Is committed to developing professionally. Takes advantage of a variety of learning activities,	

Cultural Competence	Respects and relates well to people from varied backgrounds. Sees diversity as an opportunity.
Customer/Client Focus	Makes customers/clients and their needs a primary focus. Gains customer trust and respect. Meets or exceeds customer expectations
Decision Making/Problem Solving	Makes sound, well-informed, and objective decisions. Compares data, information, and input from a variety of sources to draw conclusions.
Initiative	Takes action without being asked or required to. Achieves goals beyond job requirements.
Quality Orientation	Demonstrates a high level of care and thoroughness. Checks work to ensure completeness and accuracy.
Stress Tolerance	Maintains effective performance under pressure.
Teamwork	Participates as an active and contributing member of a team.
Work Standards	Sets high standards and well-defined, realistic goals for one's self.

Competency Rating Scale

Figure 19: Sample Competency Rating Scale

Rating	Description
-1 Unacceptable	The situation described as a positive example was inconsistent with company's definition. The example provided fell substantially short of the proficient level. In a negative example, the candidate's example suggested that no learning or development occurred from the situation.

0 Absent	The candidate was unable to provide an example.
1 Effective	The candidate demonstrated most of the indicators for successful performance in this competency. The example was relatively acceptable. The candidate could, with coaching and development, meet the competency as defined. The candidate made a few minor errors and is, therefore, less than proficient. He/she does, however, recognise his/her errors, took corrective action and learned from his/her mistakes. Development occurred and the candidate's potential for continued development is evident.
2 = Proficient	The candidate's example indicates an ability to successfully employ the knowledge, skills and abilities recquired to effectively perform this competency. The candidate's example described performance clearly and consistently. In a negative example, information was provided by the candidate that indicates learning and development has occurred from the incident.

| 3
Exceptional | The example demonstrates a very high degree of expertise in concrete measureable or observable ways. |
| | The example provided by the candidate indicates that he or she would be able to lead and train others to be excellent in the competency. |

Records

Interview Record

Airline

Application Date

Interview Date

Interview Location

Recruiters

What I did well

What I could have improved

Notes

Interview Record

Airline

Application Date

Interview Date

Interview Location

Recruiters

What I did well

What I could have improved

Notes

Interview Record

Airline   Application Date   Interview Date

Interview Location   Recruiters

What I did well

What I could have improved

Notes

Interview Record

Airline   Application Date   Interview Date

Interview Location   Recruiters

What I did well

What I could have improved

Notes

Notes

Notes

Notes

Notes

Index
Of Questions

Competencies

Customer Focus

Communication Competence

Initiative

Decision Making/Problem Solving

Teamwork & Working Relationships

Managing Adversity

Stress Tolerance

Traditional

Ice Breakers...

Personal Growth & Development...

Education...

Self Development...

Career Focus & Direction...

Work History...

Career Progression...

Cabin Crew...

Knowledge About the Job..

Suitability For the Job...

Character...

Your Views...

Other People's Views...

Stress Tolerance...

Managing Adversity...

Work Ethics...

People Skills...

Communication Competence...

Teamwork...

Analytical Skills...

Miscellaneous...

Wrap It Up...

Hypothetical

People Management...

Managing Adversity...

Lightning Source UK Ltd.
Milton Keynes UK
UKOW030321140213

206274UK00002B/63/P